CROSSINGS 17

Such Is Life

Ma la vita è fatta così

Such Is Life

Ma la vita è fatta così

Leonilde Frieri Ruberto

Translated by
Laura E. Ruberto

Introduction by
Ilaria Serra

BORDIGHERA PRESS

Library of Congress Control Number: 2009913474

Transcription from the Italian by Raffaele G. Ruberto

Cover photo: Leonilde Frieri Ruberto, Cairano (Avellino), Italy, 1949

Printed in the United States.

Published by
BORDIGHERA PRESS
John D. Calandra Italian American Institute
25 West 43rd Street, 17th Floor
New York, NY 10036

CROSSINGS 17
ISBN 978-1-59954-004-7

CONTENTS

Preface

On Translating the Orange Spiral Notebook

LAURA E. RUBERTO

In 1982, over the course of about two weeks, my paternal grand-mother—Leonilde Frieri Ruberto—wrote down some of her memories about her life both in Southern Italy and the United States.[1] My grandmother had very little formal education and was not in the least bit used to writing. And yet she filled an orange spiral notebook —the kind kids use in school—with 80 pages, mostly double-spaced, written in a steady but uncomfortable cursive. Framed more as a story she might tell her grandchildren, Nonna 'Ilde, as we called her, had written a memoir.

During those two weeks, her husband, my grandfather, and one of my aunts ("Aunt Bea") were visiting Italy; my grandmother stayed with another one of my aunts ("Aunt Tina"), on Long Island. At the time, my grandparents lived in Pittsburgh, Pennsylvania, and my two aunts lived in New York. Aunt Bea, who recently told me she always loved hearing her mother talk about her life in Italy—"I loved listening, because she seemed happy then"—had asked her to write down some of her memories. From this point on, the details of the story get a little murky. When exactly did she start writing? Where did she get the notebook? What is certain is that when my grandfather and aunt

---

[1] This project has brought together my family history and my academic work in exciting ways; as such, I want to acknowledge the support of a variety of people. I thank Anthony Julian Tamburri for first passing on the original translation of *Such Is Life* to his then-graduate student, Ilaria Serra, and for generously supporting this bilingual publication. Much gratitude goes to Ilaria Serra, with whom it has been satisfying to work, albeit virtually, on this book. Various folks offered comments and suggestions on drafts of this preface as well as aspects of the translation itself. I thank Pasquale Verdicchio, Teresa Fiore, Joseph Sciorra, and Paolo Speranza for their particular ideas and guidance. Further help, especially in relation to the use of dialect and details of family history, came from Raffaele G. Ruberto, Beatrice Ruberto, and Ernestine Franco. *Un grazie particolare* goes to Matthew Mulligan Goldstein, whose careful editor's eye and steadfast encouragement for all of my projects cannot be recognized enough.

returned from their trip, my grandparents returned to Pittsburgh, and the orange spiral notebook, now filled with my grandmother's writing, stayed behind.

For a number of years no one paid much attention to the notebook; indeed, Aunt Tina recently told me, "It took us a while to get around to reading it, probably a few years." My grandmother (she once told me that her name in the U.S. was Leonilde Ruberto and that in Italy, "where they don't care about the husband's name," it was Leonilde Frieri) had written it using a peculiar blend of standard Italian and dialect. Recognizing that the story was compelling but a challenge for some of the family and friends who might like to read it, Aunt Tina started to translate it into English, yet laid the project aside for various reasons.

As my grandmother herself describes, she repeated the fourth grade, not because she didn't pass, but because that was as much formal education as the Italian Fascist government made available in her village, and her father, a cobbler by trade and one of the better-off men in town, thought she was too young to stop attending school. Indeed, one of the many intriguing observations she makes in her story is the way in which she describes her and her fellow townspeople's unapologetic and relatively detached relationship to Fascism: "during this period fascism came and we all had to be fascists and so even I was one." It came. We did it. *Basta.*

In 1982, I turned 13. I had been to Italy about four times, mainly during the summers to visit my mother's family in Rome. I am a second-generation Italian American: my parents' emigration, as this memoir notes, is representative of a larger postwar movement of Italians from their hometowns. By 1982, I had only been to my father's hometown of Cairano once, for a few days, when I was just shy of three. It had been my first trip to the Old Country. As my grandmother remarks here, none of our family was left in Cairano, all having either emigrated or passed away. While my father returned to visit his hometown more frequently, my limited time in Italy was mainly spent with my first cousins, aunts, uncles, and grandparents in the Eternal City.

In 1992, I turned 23. Having graduated from college in California, and not quite interested in settling into any kind of routine, I decided to spend the good part of a year roaming around the globe by myself. Suffice it to say that at one point in my trip I took a three-day detour and headed to Alta Irpinia, the land-locked region east of Naples, in the province of Avellino, where Cairano sits. From the U.S. my father made arrangements for me to stay with distant relatives. I arrived at the Cairano train station after a four-hour ride from Naples (today it takes less than 90 minutes by car). My grandmother's first cousin, whom she describes in these pages when she visits her in Venezuela ("I had a cousin from both my mother's and father's side of the family"), having long returned to Italy, met me at the station. The three days were quite typical of such a visit: I would walk around a now-relatively deserted town, and I would be stopped by the older men hanging out near the only bar in town or the women crocheting in the sun or on their way to the cemetery or church.[2] Before inviting me for coffee, they would ask me who I was. Then, once they looked at my face, they would correctly identify me, usually by establishing my relationship to "Fuluccio lu furgiare" ("fuluccio the blacksmith," my great-grandfather, Raffaele Ruberto), "Runate 'r 'Nestina ("Donato son of Ernestina," Donato, my grandfather, Ernestina, my great-grandmother), or "Lionilde Ciavé" (Leonilde Ciavé, my grandmother, the author of this memoir, who was often identified by her own grandfather's nickname, Ciavé). In such a town, family trees are familiar bits of public record.

At the time of my visit, my Cairano *nonno*, Nonno Donato, had just recently passed away, but Nonna 'Ilde was alive and living in Pittsburgh, where I was born. My grandfather immigrated to the U.S., by way of Venezuela, in 1953, my grandmother and most of her children arrived in 1954, my father immigrated in 1958, and my mother, whom my father returned to Italy to marry, came to the U.S. in 1962. I had heard many stories from my *nonni* about Cairano over the course of afternoons spent in their house on South Evaline Street in Pitts-

---

[2] ISTAT census figures show how the town has been affected by continual emigration throughout the twentieth century: in 1921 Cairano's population was 1,526; in 1961, it was down to 1,269. By 1991, it was 556, and in 2007 it was 395.

burgh's Italian American neighborhood, Bloomfield (the second house Nonna 'Ilde speaks of buying). Although my family lived in the suburbs, my siblings and I were all born in Bloomfield, and we returned there often. I was fortunate to have been raised without the shame of origin of which previous generations of Italian Americans sometimes speak. Indeed, in the 1970s, American ideology embraced, or at least tried to embrace, ethnic pride and a growing sense of the benefits of multiculturalism. This visible political shift certainly aided my parents' already progressive outlook on culture; they did everything within their means to nurture in my older siblings and me an appreciation for and knowledge about Italy, its culture and history, including its language and dialects. My mother was the only one in her family to emigrate to the U.S., my Roman *nonni* and *zii* did not speak English: thus we children had no choice but to speak Italian if we wanted to communicate with them. The same was true, more or less, for Nonna 'Ilde.

Nonna 'Ilde never learned a lot of English. She mostly spoke dialect, which she would attempt to Italianize when she spoke to my mother and to sprinkle with English when she spoke to her grandchildren. In fact, the original manuscript of her memoir reads quite like I remember her talking. It is the work of someone whose relationship to language was mainly oral, rather than written, as Ilaria Serra observes in her Introduction.

In 1992, before heading back to California, I stopped in Pennsylvania and New York. It was while on Long Island visiting my aunts that I found out about the memoir's existence. Sharing stories with my aunts about my trip abroad, we inevitably turned to talking about Cairano. They had left Italy as very young girls, and they shared with me their childhood memories both of Cairano and of their first years in the U.S. It was then that Aunt Tina pulled the spiral notebook out of a drawer. I opened it to see an old-fashioned Italian-style handwriting. I immediately started reading and was instantly engrossed by Nonna 'Ilde's words, her story.

Aunt Tina also told me she had begun translating the memoir, and thus I decided to give it a try myself. By 1995, I had translated Nonna

'Ilde's story, entitling it *Such Is Life* from a phrase, "ma la vita è fatta così," she uses at the end of her story (she had not given the memoir a title). I took on the task, as my aunt had originally, in great part for the benefit of my extended family, in particular for cousins, nieces, and nephews who I knew could not read the original. It quickly became a family project, different members pitching in (with proofreading and editing, cover art, and money)—the result was a small book that is still treasured among family and close friends. When I first told Nonna 'Ilde what I was doing, her response was, "Ma perché? Why are you translating it? It's just an old woman's life." But then she was quiet and it became clear she was happy that I wanted to share her story with others.

In the original translation, my goal was mainly to make Nonna 'Ilde's words readable, accessible to her grandchildren and great-grand-children. As such, I made rather liberal changes, the most prominent being the addition of periods, commas, semicolons, and even para-graph breaks where none existed in the original. The original manu-script, as it has been meticulously transcribed here by my father, Raf-faele G. Ruberto, has neither paragraph breaks nor semicolons, lacks consistent capitalization and diacritical marks, and only features a handful of periods. In line with an oral story, her memoir reads best when it is read aloud. There are pauses, mainly in the form of commas and words such as *allora, così,* and *perché.* Serra nicely outlines some of the unique aspects of the language used in the original, but let me emphasize some points as well. In addition to her spelling being more or less phonetic renderings of her regional Italian, the original has a particularly striking way of ending many verbs and nouns. In Caira-nese, as with other Neapolitan dialects, many standard Italian words are cut off, and endings do not always correspond to a particular gend-er or case. She apparently recognized the difference between her dia-lect and standard Italian enough that she attempted to give words their proper endings. However, she didn't always get them right. When read in the original, the endings are often incorrect and will clearly appear as such to Italian readers ("perche ci volevo tanto bene," or "io non mi lamentava mai").

Throughout the English translation I have attempted to recreate much of the style and tone of the original by relying on the original word order, punctuation, and capitalization. I have not, however, purposely misspelled words, left words unfinished, or written in an otherwise incorrect English in order to evoke her incorrect Italian. Translations are, at best, rough copies. Walter Benjamin, in "The Task of the Translator," writes that "the kinship of language manifests itself in translations" (73). That is, translations, "instead of resembling the meaning of the original, must lovingly and in detail incorporate the original's mode of signification, thus making both the original and the translation recognizable as fragments of a greater language" (78). I hope to have shown here in a lovingly and detailed way some of the fragments of the language of migration, work, family, memory, and a woman's life.

To have Bordighera Press publish this bilingual version of the memoir offers her words a permanence and a significance that I imagine Nonna 'Ilde would have never quite understood. Moreover, that I have been able to work with Ilaria Serra on this project, and that she offers a contextual grounding of the work within the realm of Italian American women's memoir, is especially significant to me as a scholar of Italian American culture. Serra's Introduction offers a broader context within which to read the memoir, establishing its cultural value beyond the familial realm for which it was originally intended. In introducing her study on Italian women's autobiography, *Public History, Private Stories*, Graziella Parati discusses the relationship writing has to space, all the while recognizing the "problematic points of contact between private and public":

> The public act of writing a private life is the locus where women writers can seek to come to terms with the still contradictory relationship between the role of women in the public and private spheres. (2-3)

Serra's Introduction complicates this relationship between the assumed private and public space recounted within *Such Is Life*, recognizing how the push of emigration and the pull of immigration compel the recounting of particular stories of one woman's relationship to her surroundings.

My grandfather died on December 1, 1991, at the age of 81. For a few years Nonna 'Ilde continued to live in Pittsburgh, but eventually she moved to Long Island to be near her daughters. She passed away there on October 17, 2000, a few hours before I was to board a plane to New York (where I was to visit her and present at a university conference on Italian immigration). Instead, I flew from Oakland, California, to Pittsburgh, Pennsylvania, as her body traveled from New York to Pittsburgh as well. It was a route she had taken practically 46 years earlier when she first arrived to the United States, apprehensive but looking towards a new life, with big dreams for her children, and, as I've always imagined, for herself as well.

WORKS CITED

Parati, Graziella. *Public History, Private Stories: Italian Women's Autobiography.* Minneapolis, Minnesota: University of Minnesota Press, 1996.

Benjamin, Walter. "The Task of the Translator." *Illuminations: Essays and Reflections.* New York: Schocken Books, 1968.

Introduction

Ilaria Serra

Parable of a life; river of words; footprint of a woman's existence: these are some of the ways we might define Leonilde Frieri Ruberto's autobiography, a precious and rare example of a life-story written by an Italian immigrant woman. If first-person accounts of "ordinary" immigrants are very rare, those specifically of women can be counted on the fingers of one hand. Only one, written in Italian, has been published in Italy: *Il calicanto non cresce a Chicago* by Amabile Peguri Santacaterina.[1] None to date has been published here in the United States.

If we make a head count of first-generation Italian women autobiographers,[2] we can better understand the importance of this book. As of now, we can count two as-told-to autobiographies: *Rosa. The Life of an Italian Immigrant* by Rosa Cavalleri, edited by Marie Hall Ets; and *My Mother: Memoir of a Sicilian Woman* that Giuseppina Liarda Macaluso narrated to her son, Mario Macaluso. We then find two life-stories written as a "shared" story, almost ancillary to a man's life-story: Bruna Pieracci wrote her about her life as a background to the remembrance of her father, a Modenese miner of Iowa;[3] the Jewish Anna Yona from Turin, picked up the pen after her husband, David, died and left his *memoirs* unfinished (the manuscript is still unpublished).[4] Other Italian women wrote their unpublished stories of im-

---

[1] The book was published by La Serenissima, a small publishing house in Vicenza; Amabile Santacaterina's hometown is Chiuppano, in the province of Vicenza.

[2] For first generation, I mean the generation that came to the United States, not the one born here. Italian American autobiographies by women of second and third generation are more common, and critical accounts of these can be found in the works by Edvige Giunta's *Writing with an Accent* and Caterina Romeo's *Narrativa tra le due sponde*.

[3] Bruna Pieracci's work is included in Salvatore LaGumina's book *The Immigrants Speak*; and Maria Parrino includes it in her dissertation about autobiographies of Italian American women.

[4] The unpublished manuscript is preserved in the Immigration History Research Center of Saint Paul (MN).

migration, but they cannot be compared to Ruberto. Two of them
spent only a period of their life, even if a long period, in the United
States: Elisabeth Evans and Elvezia Marcucci, while a third one, Maria
Bottiglieri was a war-bride.[5] To my knowledge, these are the only available autobiographies by Italian immigrant women.[6]

Several factors make autobiographies by Italian immigrant wom-
en a rarity: many of them were illiterate, or if they knew how to read
they would have never thought of being capable of writing more than
letters home. Too many had no time to write and almost all never
even imagined of writing about themselves. For Mary Frances Pipino
Italian women's autobiography is "oxymoronic": Italian immigrant
society was male-dominated (even if mother-centered, as Rudolph Vecoli points out in "Contadini in Chicago"), and women are the last link
of the "lost generation" of immigrants that Giuseppe Prezzolini la-
ments in his *I trapiantati*.

A PLACE IN LIFE

Leonilde Frieri Ruberto was 70 years old when she sat at a table
in Long Island, and started to write her life. She was the uneasy guest
of her daughter Ernestina, as she says in her last words, and since her
husband was visiting Italy, she carved out some time of her own and
wrote her story, prompted by her other daughter Beatrice. The occa-
sion of such writing is quite interesting: had her husband not gone to
Italy, and had her stay with Ernestina not been so uneasy (she writes
that the days seem all the same because she cannot go to mass on
Sunday), perhaps Ruberto would have never written her story. She
would have been like thousands of other immigrant women, too busy,

---

[5]These unpublished manuscripts are preserved in the Archivio Diaristico Nazionale of Pieve
Santo Stefano (AR).
[6]I would like to acknowledge the autobiography of an Italian immigrant to Australia, Adele
Bentley (neé Levis) who migrated at the age of one, from Belluno to Perth, in 1927: *Between
two Cultures: Italian-Australian. An Autobiography*. The seventy-years old Bentley looks back at
her life, from the bag hut in the Australian Balcatta, a rural town, to her integrated life as an
Australian lady looking at kookaburras, possums and joeys in her backyard. "Growing up in
Australia meant growing up in a society –not just watching change, but about *'being change'*.
Our family was a still is part of that struggle. . . . and what am I? One thing is now clear, I am
an Australian of Italian descent. Australia is my home" (161-62).

too preoccupied with their husband, house chores and daily mass, to even think of writing. Interestingly the inspiration to write her autobiography is born from a second, smaller, deracination and discomfort. We know that the original situation that often triggers an autobiography is a troubled feeling of not-belonging, the experience of a revolution. Whenever existence betrays, the individual seems to find comfort and balance by concentrating on his/her own presence on this earth. Ruberto is actually curing a long-lasting discomfort, but finally picks up the pen in a situation that vaguely resembles her original anxiety of immigration.

The autobiography opens on a spatial note: Ruberto was born in Cairano, in the Province of Avellino, a little agricultural town. Her first desire is to create and identity and set her personal space: clearly, she is trying to repair her own displacement. Healing the flow of time by pinning down cardinal dates is important, as we shall see, but her first move is spatial: as the immigrant women of Helen Barolini's important novel, *Umbertina*, she firstly needs to find her place on earth.[7] This need finds a confirmation in the ending of her story that also closes on an indication of space: she is temporarily in Long Island, but she soon will go back to Pittsburgh where her life will settle back into its comfortable routine. Pittsburgh is the place she calls home now, however many losses she suffered from being there. She quickly synthesizes such losses in the dramatic close of her story: "anchio lasciai mio padre e tutti i miei cari per non vederli mai piu" ("even I left my father and all my dear ones never to see them again"). Her writing is not mainly aimed at healing the passing of time, as a common autobiography would, but rather to mend her inner geographical map, that has been torn by immigration. This writer's *ethos* is that of an immigrant; her autobiography will recover the past in order to find her own place, a promised land of the mind.

---

[7] Helen Barolini calls this the immigrant's *quaquaversal* identity in *Umbertina*. The book traces the steps of Tina backward to her great-grandmother's hometown in Calabria, in the hope of finding her own "place."

THE GRINDING OF TIME

Unlike Estelle Jelinek's description of woman's autobiography,[8] Ruberto's story is absolutely vertical and chronologically ordered. Here are Ruberto's temporal milestones. She takes good care to note day, month and year: her birth (January 2, 1913); her brother's birth (March 23, 1915) and the start of World War I (May 24, 1915); her sister's birth (December 28, 1920); her mother's death (March 3, 1934); her wedding (January 3, 1935); her son Raffaele's birth (April 21, 1937), her son Peppino's birth (April 19, 1939); her father in law's death (February 27, 1943); her husband's return as a prisoner of war (October 5, 1945); her daughter Beatrice's birth (July 31, 1946) and that of her daughter Ernestina (November 16, 1948); her husband's first letter from America (December 18, 1953), her own departure for the United States (November 30, 1954); her husband's work accident (November 27, 1957); her brother Angelo's death (October 14, 1958); her father's death (November 22, 1964), her brother Michelangelo's death (May 3, 1965), her sister Assunta's death (November 19, 1969).

Of these nineteen turning points, six are births, six are deaths, two are events related to immigration: a letter and her departure. The life of this woman ran parallel to History, touched by two World Wars and Immigration, but mainly tied to her family's courtyard. It is a familial, private time, not a public one. Her life draws a parable: it ebbs through all the family additions, and it wanes through the painful string of deaths. She is the only one who remains of her immediate family, and this loneliness is perhaps one of the main themes of her—often sorrowful—autobiography.

RESIGNATION AND WORK

What is the final balance of an immigrant life? "Un po' buono un po' brutto" Ruberto repeats four times: good and bad went side by side. But the upheaval of emigration leaves a deep scar in her soul. Until the

---

[8]In "Women's Autobiography and the Male Tradition," Jelinek reacts against the erasing of women's autobiography from literary criticism, and gives a few guiding principles to consider women's work and style. Among her observations she writes: "Irregularity rather than orderliness informs the self portraits of women" (17).

end her heart never settles, she remains nostalgic and resigned. Resignation is the common element of many Italian "ordinary" autobiographers. While the successful ones wrote their self-building through their victories, the "ordinary" ones—the great majority of Italian immigrants, those who did not become neither famous nor millionaires —wrote their surviving through their losses.[9] For these, resignation is their guiding star. "Ci voleva solo la rassegnazione," Ruberto writes. *Rassegnazione, mi rassegnai, ci rassegnammo*: the word appears in every form. In the same way, Ruberto treats "disgrace" as a guest, a personal acquaintance who knocks at her door, coming and going at pleasure: "ma la sfortuna venne" and later, "venne la disgrazia." Nothing can be done against it. She can only open the door. The personification of Fortuna and Sfortuna are common in Italian literature, starting with Machiavelli's *Prince*, but also commonly used by the general population. In particular, immigrant autobiographers treat her, Lady Misfortune, as a travel companion. Curiously, both the autobiographies of Ruberto and Santacaterina end with the same sentence that spews resignation: Ruberto writes "la vita e' fatta cosi'," and Santacaterina echoes "questa e' la vita!"

The second aspect that Ruberto's autobiography shares with "ordinary" autobiography is the centrality of work. Work, work, work. Immigrants worked, and women did their share. Ruberto belonged to a well-off family of peasants who owned their fields and hired labor. She did not have a public job ("il mestiero" she calls it, with a hyper-masculinization of the term "mestiere," that indicates that it was part of the male world. The word has to arrive in America, where women started to work outside the home more frequently, to become feminine, with another linguistic hybrid: "la jobba"!). She nevertheless always worked hard in her house, as a mother for the family, after her own mother was immobilized by disease. Young Ruberto helped in the fields, brought food to the workers, sold fertilizer and wine for her father, and collected the production from their fields. After her wedding, she worked as a seamstress, and twice supported her own

---

[9]For a systematic description of such autobiographies, see Ilaria Serra's *The Value of Worthless Lives. Writing Italian Immigrant Autobiography.*

family alone, in the absence of her husband: during the war and during his migration to Venezuela and the United States. In these occasions she reveals the heroism of Italian women who remained "tutte sole," and worked twice as much sharing their solidarity ("continuammo a essere sempre insieme," "si aiutavamo uno con l'altro"). When her husband left for Venezuela, she shows to be perfectly aware of her own heroism: "mi lasco con 4 figli, adesso era sola e dovette fare tutto come quando cera la guerra dovevo lavorare in campagna, e dovevo accudire 4 figli, non due."

Unlike many other immigrant women, Ruberto does not find a job outside the house once she arrives in the United States. We can assume that she continues to work as a seamstress, but she does so from home. She never reaches that independence that many women experience once in America. She remains inside the family, perhaps hindered by her ignorance of English, or perhaps because she was not economically forced to find a job outside the home.[10] This does not take away from her hard work, and at the end, work is what synthesizes her entire existence: "o tanto lavorato o avuto tanti dispiaceri."

A STRONG WOMAN

From the facts recounted, we could imagine Ruberto as a woman attached to the family and submissive to it. Ruberto's life turns all around her family, and her extended family. Also her parents-in-law become part of her life. On one hand she prefers to keep them at a distance—as when she, together with her husband, break the local custom that wants the last son living in his parents' home, and moves out with her husband—on the other hand, she later counts on her mother-in-law's help when her husband leaves, and grows very attached to her.[11]

---

[10] See Maddalena Tirabassi's article "Un mondo alla rovescia: le emigrate italiane negli Stati Uniti da contadine a cittadine" in *Annali dell'Istituto Alcide Cervi* (1990).

[11] For this attachment, sometimes servitude to the in-laws, see the letters that Emilio Franzina cites in his "Donne emigranti e donne di emigranti. Memorie e scritture popolari dell'emigrazione femminile italiana fra i due secoli," *Annali dell'Istituto Alcide Cervi.*

The way she describes her engagement can leave the reader to imagine she accepted, rather than chose, her husband, as an obedient daughter. In an anti-romantic way, Ruberto leaves no space in her autobiography for courtship and love making, perhaps due to the custom of Italian "good girls," exactly the opposite of what happens in the autobiography of Maria Bottiglieri, the war bride. We can notice, for one, that she does not give her husband's name, and the description of his courtship is quite brutal: "cera un ragazzo che i suoi genitori volevano per me ... ed e proprio questo che mi sono sposato." From her words we can understand that the 21-year-old Ruberto would have preferred to live unattached with her girlfriends, none of whom had a fiancé, but she obeyed her parents' decisions.

This should not lead us to imagine a passive Ruberto. Let us remember that she stands up for herself on at least three other occasions: when she leaves her parents-in-law house, when she refuses to join her husband in Venezuela (although this was prompted at least in part by feelings she had about her children's wellbeing), and when she refuses to accompany him on his return trip to Italy. Even if she describes her position in a dense web of familial relations, she still concentrates on herself, not on her father, husband or children. A family woman, she still remains the queen of her story.

THE UPROOTING

Emigration has no appeal for this woman. Ruberto is forced to leave, and she shows none of the anticipation, the thirst for knowledge, the drive toward the new that sometimes sweetens the recounts of immigration. Venezuela does not have any attraction ("dicevano che non era buono, il clima era troppo caldo la gente era cattiva si diceva che vivevano come selvaggi era tutto diferente da noi ma si diceva di azzardare"). "Io non volle andare": Ruberto stood up to her husband and refused to follow him. But after four years, she had no choice and she had to leave for New York.

The absence of stereotypical descriptions of the awesome city and the richness of the new land strikes the reader. Absence here is louder than presence, and it speaks of her incomplete adaptation. The usual fairytale descriptions of the lighted New York skyline do not appear in Ruberto's memories. Her "compliments" to the city, minimal at best, do not take up more space than "certo che nel vedere NY. era per noi come un paradiso." Her life in Pittsburgh is more comfortable than in Italy, but "non era un granche." Her heart is elsewhere, as she confesses: "si stava molto meglio, ma io pensavo sempre ai miei che avevo restato in Italia." "Il pensiero dell'Italia" is alleviated only by the arrival of her son Raffaele, whom she had left behind in order for him to finish high school.

The counting down of Ruberto's life is accompanied by the disappearance of her family members, something extremely sad and heartfelt, as in this sentence that accumulates short cries of loss: "mi mise a piangere era finita la mia famiglia non aveva piu nessuno tutti morti." The death of her family means the death of an entire world, be it her youth or her town's reality. Death becomes the face of the old country, and Ruberto refuses to go back to Italy because she is afraid of seeing the change: "io non volle andare erano tutti morti." The sense of loss envelops her and kills her soul too: "mi sentivo morta pure con loro."

The internal fight to go back to Italy and face the change takes up a large portion of the drama in her autobiography. The act of returning is charged with meanings of revelation, crude discovery and facing the bitter truth. Twenty years she waits before finding the courage to go back, but in Cairano she only visits cemeteries. Everything has changed. This same theme is curiously dramatized by Antonio dal Masetto, an Italian-Argentinian novelist who tells the story of Agata's return to Italy, in terms similar to how Ruberto must have felt it. He describes Agata's thoughts in front of her childhood house, and we can imagine, in turn, Ruberto in her home town:

> Agata, sorpresa, guardava e tardava o si rifiutava d'identificarla. Avrebbe voluto dire di no, avrebbe voluto non riconoscerla, perché in qualche modo, dolorosamente non era la sua casa. Ma era lei. . . . L'unica cosa presente in lei era il disincanto. Aveva tardato a riaversi, sentiva il peso della stanchezza e allo stesso tempo provava la sensazione di aver appena commesso un errore, di aver visto ciò che non doveva vedere e adesso non

avrebbe più potuto fare marcia indietro. Si—aveva ammesso—è questa. (86-87)[12]

This is the moment when Ruberto feels the last root give way: "non piansi quando partii dall'italia per tornare in america tanto non lasciavo nessuno." We can imagine that after such a trip, the obsession with Italy has finally left her. But it is not so. Her writing betrays her. When she tells us that she refused to accompany her husband in his visit to Italy, she explains that she did not want to go visit graves. And then, the Cairano of her memory reappears, like a ray of light in the dark, the only poetic description in such a practical recount of life. She depicts the imagined hometown that did not leave her, until this day, and indirectly tells us all the pain of her divided soul:

e meglio che ricordo il mio paese come lo lasciai 28 anni fa, bello pulito ridente su una collina 815 metro al livello del mare con unaria pulita e chiara che da un lato al mattino ce l'aurora quando sorgeva il sole e alla sera al tramonto il sole calava con quei raggio di fuoco, e alla notte la luna con le stelle che brillavano erano cosi chiare li contavamo sempre quando eravamo bambini, sono 28 anni che mi trovo qui in America non ho mai potuto vedere il cielo azzurro con il sole che splende pulito e neanche ho mai visto la notte bella con la luna chiare e le stelle, alla primavera quando arrivavano a migliaia le rondini dalle parti calde con il loro canto come se volessero dire siamo arrivate, e in autunno quando si mettevano in fila sui fili eletrici col loro canto per dirci arrivederci all'anno prossimo per poi ripartire di nuovo ai luoghi caldi, perche da noi veniva l'inverno, il mio paese era povero ma bello.

The strength of her denial is perfectly clear to her, who buries herself in her private limpid Cairano, and refuses to know the present of her town and the news her husband will take to her: "ma e meglio a non saperlo." Her last sentence, already mentioned, does nothing but

---

[12]Antonio dal Masetto was born in Intra in 1938 and migrated to Argentina in 1950. This passage is from *La Tierra Incomparable*, and it is quoted in Camilla Cattarulla's book *L'azzardo e la pazienza* (86).

reinforce the sense of bitter loss that flavors her life: "lasciai mio padre e tutti i miei cari per non vederli mai piu."

Ruberto may have adapted to the new soil, but not completely. Deracination has taken place, through one strong pull. Her roots have expanded in the new land, yet her lust for life has changed color forever. She experiences the "double absence" that Abdelmalek Sayad defines in his book: absence both from her old and her new country. Merriness belongs to her youth in Italy, to the pic-nics with her girlfriends and the pilgrimages to the Churches. In America she found the good life, but she lost the light laughter of youth. Following the metaphor of the tree, Amabile Santacaterina lucidly describes the *malaise* she shares with Ruberto—and probably many other immigrant women: "Forse, io sono come il calicanto che non cresce a Chicago" (22).

STYLISTIC OBSERVATIONS

From a comparison with the only other female immigrant autobiography, Amabile Santacaterina's *Il calicanto*, we can infer a main characteristic of Ruberto's style. Her life belongs to the past as its narrative is all told in the past tense, in line with oral story telling traditions. While Santacaterina—a true exception—tells her life with the urgency of the present tense, showing that everything is still stirring and clear in her mind (and filling up hundreds of pages) with a noon-like hot narration, Ruberto tells a more pacified story, a work of the sunset. Her life is over and gone, and she can only recover it through recollection. The labor of memory appears more than once in her observations: "mi ho dimenticato di dire" or "io non so raccontare tutto" when she cannot say what happened to her husband during the war. Again, toward the end, she writes: "ci sono tante cose che con la mente me le ricordo, ma non le so scrivere." Her mind is strained in the effort of memory, and she often feels inadequate.

Ruberto's description of her life in Italy takes place under the sign of *negation*. It was different *then*, nothing like *now*. She seems to have her readers clear in her mind, and helps them in the effort of imagining *another* world. She seems to be warning them: you have to imagine a place devoid of all commodities that are here today, in the United States: "non vi era acqua potabile ... non cerano panetteria ... non cera luce eletrica"; "non cerano mai giocattoli mai bambole ... le usanze di festegiare ne compleanni, ne onomastichi, e neanche cerano i regali di Natale"; "non cerano ne cappotti ... non cerano guanti." Further, "non avevamo altre divertimenti non cera niente ne cinemo non si usciva mai, non si dava retta a nessun ragazzo ... mai si usciva di sera non cerano radio non televisione." Through this long series of "non" and "mai," Ruberto wants to make sure her American grand-children know the difference.

Another proof that this writer has her audience clear in her mind is found toward the end. When her prose becomes more comfortable, she addresses directly her readers with oral cadences: "immagginate se avesse successo una disgrazia," and "forse non credete," and finally "non credete che io lo [Cairano] volli lasciare con piacere."

Another narrative technique that Ruberto employs is listing. She often makes lists to faithfully detail how life happened, following the wavy movement of memory. Thus she makes a list of Christmas sweets: "i dolci le sfogliatelle le zeppole i strufoli." She unrolls the list of pasta that she had learned to make: "i cavatelli i fusilli i gnocchi e cappelletti e la sfoglia per fare le tagliatelle." And she draws a menu of the food people used to eat: "spesso portavano gli uccelli lepre e altre animale che prendevano portavano pescie che pescavano uova e tante altre cose." She also lists the wedding gifts from her husband's family: "una bella collana un orologio a bracciale una spilla tutto oro." By not leaving any stone unturned, though a systematic catalogue, Ruberto makes sure she is complete and thorough in her narration.

Ruberto's language is dry and effective, anti-rhetorical and con-crete. She steers away from any moral preaching (only at the end she almost slips into one: "il mondo e campiato ..."). She sticks to facts and factual descriptions, she does not concede to poetry or philosophical reflections. Like many other "ordinary" autobiographers, coming from a material culture, she tells a material life. These writers know that they have nothing to teach, but they can give testimony. And, like many of them, she affixes the seal of truth to her story "questo che ho detto dallinizio e tutto vero."

Even if not studying longer than fourth grade, she embroiders her language effectively. She uses a standard Italian, not completely but quite correct, with some echoes of Southern dialectal phonetics in the labial consonants (*inbastava* for *impastava*, *rombevo* for *rompevo*), and in the dental consonants (*candina* for *cantina, correto* and *corretino* for *corredo* and *corredino*). She slips into Ital-English only a handful of times, like when she writes "quel poco di fornitura" for "furniture" (*mobili* in Italian), and mentions Peppino going "alle ai scuola" (high school). This makes us think that she probably never mastered English —as many other women who, as Ruberto notices, could live without having to learn the new language: "al quartiere dove eravamo noi erano quasi tutti Italiani." This should not surprise: many Italian immigrants did not learn English even after thirty years of work here. They did not have time to go to school for foreigners, and most of all, dealt almost exclusively with Italian co-workers, bosses, and clients. The result is that they spoke phonetic English, by repeating the sounds but not knowing how words were written.

The original manuscript, as her granddaughter Laura E. Ruberto found it, looks like almost one long sentence. Her prose flows like an unstoppable river. She appears to have never (or seldom) read back (as we can gather by her "non so se ho detto che ho la pressione alta," when indeed she had). She is just transported forward by the strong current of narration. There are very few periods and no paragraph separations. The effect is perhaps not wanted, but striking: even the style speaks here, metaphorically, of the writer's will to keep everything together, to mold her life into a compact solid, and thus to counterbalance the shredding effect of migration and time. Now that "non ce e restato piu nessuno," Ruberto at 70, is only waiting for her days to count down. She is almost surprised to have lived this long (unlike most of her family who died young), and muses at the "sentence" of her life, as Lawrence Ferlighetti writes, in his poem "The Old Italians Dying:" "The old men are waiting / for it to be finished / for their glorious sentence on earth / to be finished" (137).

WORKS CITED

Barolini, Helen. *Umbertina*, New York: Seaview Books, 1979.

Bentley, Adele. *Between Two Cultures: Italian-Australian. An Autobiography.* Roleystone, Western Australia: Gosnells Print, 1996.

Bottiglieri, Maria. *Sposa di guerra.* Typescript. Archivio Diaristico Nazionale of Pieve Santo Stefano, 1986.

Cattarulla, Camilla and Ilaria Magnani. *L'azzardo e la pazienza. Donne emigrate nella narrative argentina.* Troina: Citta' Aperta Edizioni, 2004.

Dal Masetto, Antonio. *La tierra incomparable.* Buenos Aires: Editorial Planeta Argentina, 1994.

Ets, Mary Hall. *Rosa: The Life of an Italian Immigrant.* Minneapolis: University of Minnesota Press, 1970.

Evans, Elisabeth. *Un attimo una vita.* Typescript, Archivio Diaristico Nazionale of Pieve Santo Stefano, 1996.

Ferlinghetti, Lawrence. "The Old Italians Dying." *From the Margin. Writings in Italian Americana.* Ed. Anthony Julian Tamburri, Paolo Giordano, Fred Gardaphe. West Lafayette, IN: Pur due University Press, 2000. 135-38.

Franzina, Emilio. "Donne emigranti e donne di emigranti. Memorie e scritture popolari dell'emigrazione femminile italiana fra i due secoli." *Annali dell'Istituto Alcide Cervi,* 12/1990. 237-264.

Giunta, Edvige. *Writing with an Accent: Contemporary Italian American Women Authors.* New York: Palgrave, 2002.

Jelinek, Estelle. "Women's Autobiography and the Male Tradition." Jelinek, Estelle, ed. *Women's Autobiography: Essays in Criticism.* Bloomington: Indiana University Press, 1980. 1-20.

Macaluso, Giuseppina Liarda. *My Mother. Memoir of a Sicilian Woman.* Trans. Ed Mario Macaluso. New York: EPI, 1998.

Marcucci, Elvezia. *Le memorie di una novantenne smemorata (che sarei io).* Manuscript. Archivio Diaristico Nazionale of Pieve Santo Stefano, 2001.

Parrino, Maria. *Il luogo della memoria e il luogo dell'identita: narrazioni autobiografiche di donne dell'immigrazione italo-americana.* Unpublished dissertation, Genova, 1988.

Pieracci, Bruna. "Bruna Pieracci." LaGumina, Salvatore. *The Immigrants Speak.* New York: Center for Immigration Studies, 1979. 33-47.

Prezzolini, Giuseppe, *I trapiantati*, Milano: Longanesi, 1963.

Romeo, Caterina. *Narrative tra due sponde : memoir di italiane d'America.* Roma: Carocci, 2005.

Santacaterina Amabile, Peguri. *Il calicanto non cresce a Chicago.* Vicenza: La Serenissima, 1992.

Sayad, Abdelmalek. *La doppia assenza. Dalle illusioni dell'emigrato alle sofferenze dell'immigrato.* Ed. Salvatore Palidda. Milano: Raffaello Cortina Editore, 2002.

Serra, Ilaria. *The Value of Worthless Lives. Writing Italian Immigrant Autobiography.* New York: Fordham University Press, 2007.

Tirabassi, Maddalena. "Un mondo alla rovescia: le emigrate italiane negli Stati Uniti da contadine a cittadine." *Annali dell'Istituto Alcide Cervi,* 12/1990. 307-323.

Vecoli, Rudolph. "Contadini in Chicago: a Critique of the Uprooted." *The Journal of American History.* Vol. 51, n. 3 (Dec. 1964). 404-417.

Yona, Anna, and David Yona. Memoires. Typescript, 1971. Immigration History Research Center, Saint Paul (MN).

Such Is Life

Such Is Life

Leonilde Frieri Ruberto

my village was small, 1500 inhabitants, it was called Cairano in
the province of Avellino, townspeople and farmers all worked
their lands, the townspeople, even though they had a trade,
cultivated their land, and the farmers sometimes worked their
own land and sometimes worked the land for the townspeople in
order to earn money for those things they had to buy, there
were few *signori* rich in land who could have sharecroppers, I
was born January 2, 1913, my father was a shoemaker and my
mother a housewife, I had a brother who was two years older
than me, and then there were my grandparents, my mother's
father was alone, my grandmother had died before I was born,
we did not make old people live by themselves, my mother had
four sisters and so my grandfather stayed four months with each
of his daughters, who counting my mother were five, my
grandfather worked at the municipal office he brought the tax
papers to the people, the municipal office sent the tax notices
by hand not by mail, my father still had both of his parents, but
then my grandmother died, and so my father's father had to do
the same thing, my father had two brothers and their father
stayed with each of them for a while, when he stayed at our
house he would always tell us stories about ghosts, about how
Jesus Christ came to this world, he didn't work any longer, he
was too old, he used to work his land, but now his sons had
divided it among themselves on March 23, 1915 my brother
Angelo was born I was a little more than two years old, then, in
the month of May, May 24, the first war broke out, and soon
after my father was called to the war, the war lasted three years,
I began to understand things I remember that when I was 3 years

old I went to the school for the little ones run by the nuns, all the children of the soldiers who were drafted ate at the government cafeteria and we played only my brother Michelangelo and I went, Angelo was too small and could not go, during the war my mother worked a lot, she had 3 children and sometimes one grandfather and sometimes the other one, and then there was the land, I've forgotten to say that my father besides being a shoemaker also had some land, that is fields and vineyards, sharecroppers worked the fields, my parents worked some on the vineyards and they hired day workers to help with the heavy work, all of this work my mother had to now with the help of women day workers because all the men were away at war, and so I also had to help out, my mother would take me with her when she went out to the fields, I would rock my little brother and watch that he didn't hurt himself and so as I said before my mother worked a lot and her strength slowly began to fail her, she wasn't able to do so much work and she didn't feel well, she didn't take care of herself but she got by, she had an older sister zia Colomba who helped her a lot, because her husband hadn't gone to war because he was old, they loved us a lot they had no children, during the war my mother never cooked she always made us eat bread with something on it because my father was in the war, but zia Colomba always brought us something to eat, they raised pigeons, chickens, and rabbits and once in a while she would bring us one of these cooked, then the war ended in 1918 my father returned and everything began as before I was over six years old and I went to school to first grade all the children who had been with the nuns knew the alphabet and could draw. my father had many people to make shoes for, with the money he earned he bought more fields and vineyards and put many workers to work on them on December 28, 1920 my sister Assunta was born I was 7 years old I was happy that I now had a

sister I would rock her clean her and play with her during this
time my grandfather died that is my mother's father we felt his
absence because he loved us very much he used to take us with
him when he made the rounds in the village delivering the tax
notices to the people but after a while my mother fell ill again
but this time it wasn't tiredness but loss of weight my father
took her to the village doctor and even to those of the
surrounding villages and no one could tell what was the matter,
but then she went to Naples to see specialists and after all the
tests they said that her blood didn't circulate well and her nerves
had constricted and she had apoplexy there was nothing to be
done her hands were already paralyzed and they sent her to the
baths every year so that her condition wouldn't worsen and so
for me everything changed I was growing but I was still little for
certain things I had to go to school, as I've said my village did
not have many conveniences there was no drinkable water we
had to go to the fountain outside of town in order to wash
clothes, there was no bakery to buy bread everyone made their
own and it was taken to the oven to be baked, there was no
electric light we used oil lamps, my mother taught me to do
many things she would tell me what needed to be done and I
would do it sometimes her younger sister zia Antonia would
come I would watch zia Antonia make bread and so then I
started to make bread for us but my hands were small and so I
had to knead a little at a time. once in a while my cousin who
lived nearby would come and help me, once I remember that my
father helped me, there were no washing machines to wash the
laundry, we had to wash clothes almost every day because of my
little sister, there was a woman whom my mother knew who
went to the fountain every day to wash clothes for the *signori*
in town, and so my mother paid her so that I could go after
school with my pail of laundry, this woman would help me and
would watch me wash the clothes, not only did my mother pay

her but she always gave her something to eat, I never complained about my situation, I never had toys I never had dolls my sister was my doll and I played with her I remember that in my village as I said in the beginning we didn't know anything maybe all of the villages in southern Italy were like this, they didn't celebrate birthdays or name days, there weren't even gifts on Christmas, it was a big holiday there were services in church and people talked about la Befana, on christmas eve parents would put stockings on the fireplace and would put fruit or chocolate candies inside them if you had been good, but if you had been bad they would put coal and ashes, I remember that I was always good, my mother and all her sisters and sisters-in-law prepared sweets sfogliatelle zeppole strufoli and other things and everyone ate together and everyone did the same thing, I remember that zia Colomba gave me something dried that looked like a rose and told me to put it in water on christmas eve if on Christmas morning it was open and had bloomed it meant that the new year would be good, it was called the rose of Jerusalem in the morning my cousins came over to see that it had opened up and we were all happy, now even my other grandfather died, but not at my house, at zio Pietro's, and we did not feel his absence so much. time passed I was 10 years old my older brother was 12 he had finished elementary school and he went away to study with the dominican Fathers in Arezzo, and so we were now fewer in the family and there was less work for me to do, I was in 4th grade and was doing well at school they taught us how to do many things, they taught us how to pull the threads close to the fabric in order to make a hem-stitch [*punto a giorno*], they made us sew hems, and many other embroidery stitches that I liked a lot, even at home, when I had time, I would practice them, my mother was teaching me how to work with the crochet hook, I was now 11 years old and about to finish school, but my father begged the teacher to let

me repeat a year that is grade 4 because I was too small to leave
school, and there were no grades higher than the fourth in our
village during this period fascism came and we all had to be
fascists and so even I was one people my age were called *piccole
Italiane*, we wore uniforms and there were many parades I had a
good time and I had many girlfriends, but after school I was very
busy helping my mother do the housework in the evening I did
my homework, and the days passed, I remember that I had a
habit of always breaking things, a day never passed that I didn't
break a dish or a glass, I broke so many glass shades of the oil
lamps, my mother loved me but sometimes she would yell at me
and tell me to be careful, as I've already said in school I was
learning a lot of needlework stitches but I still had others to
learn little by little I learned to embroider very well by hand,
school was over now, I didn't have to study anymore and I had
more time I was older now and it fell to me to do heavier work
as I've said we had vineyards and there were many workers who
tilled the fields these men who were never less than 10 11 had
to be fed they had to eat twice a day and my mother would cook
for them one of the wives of these men would come to take the
basket of food out to them my mother who as I said couldn't go
out to the fields herself, would prepare a smaller basket for me
to carry, but these heavy chores came during the winter it was
cold and there were no coats we used shawls instead there were
no gloves and to keep my hands warm my mother would wrap
small kitchen towels around my hands and in this way my hands
would stay warm while I held the basket on my head, of course
this didn't happen often, so now that I was 13 14 years old I
had to learn to sew because in my village almost all the girls
except the farm girls had to know something about sewing my
mother felt bad that I wasn't as free as the other girls who went
to learn how to sew and she wanted me to go to the seamstress
at all costs, I had a cousin the daughter of one of my father's

brothers who was a seamstress and so my mother begged her to teach me how to sew of course I couldn't go every day like the other girls, but when I went I put myself completely into it and so I could keep up with the other girls who went every day, when my friends would see me arrive they were happy, I was also happy to be with them, and they would ask me if I were coming the next day so that we could do something special together, and everyone would bring something and we would have a special little lunch it always fell to me to bring the wine my cousin would let us use the kitchen because her mother was out at the fields, her father was in America, and we would always do this when my cousin was in a good mood, sometimes she was in a bad mood, one day she was angry because there was so much work to do she had so many clients and when there was a feast day, we would even work late into the evening one day I didn't go to sew it was winter and there was snow and the girls who had gone to sew went as usual to the *castello*[1] at noon for a few minutes to get some fresh air, and that day they saw a chicken lost in the snow they grabbed it and brought it to an old woman who lived near my cousin and this woman always helped us hide the things we would bring to cook, she killed the chicken for us, that evening one of my friends came to my house to tell my mother that the next day I had to go to sew because there was so much to be done, and the next morning when I arrived they told me about the chicken, we cooked it with some pasta we did this sort of thing often, now I was a young woman and everything seemed easy the housework, washing, baking bread, one day however the bread did not want to rise and when I brought it to the oven the baker screamed at me and she said

---

[1]Cairano is a hilltown; on the highest point of the village there was once a castle (some remains are still visible and excavations have recently started to uncover the rest of it), and today that part of the village is still called *il castello*.

that I wasn't good at anything, I started to cry a neighbor was
there and she reproached the baker saying that I had made bread
since I was small and that it was uncalled for to make me cry
because bread didn't come out right even for adults sometimes,
we always made pasta by hand, it was only bought occasionally,
my mother had taught me how to make cavatelli fusilli gnocchi
cappelletti and the sheet of dough for tagliatelle, but the sheet
of dough was a little difficult to make, I remember one time that
my mother was at the baths and my father was in the fields and
I wanted to make tagliatelle and they were not coming out right
and I started to cry I didn't know what to do right then one of
my cousins passed by our house and she helped me make them
now even my brother Angelo had finished school and he had to
start learning a trade he chose cabinetmaking and my sister was
also going to school now even they did some things around the
house I remember that during this period the missionaries came
to preach for 15 days, my village was very religious and
everyone went to listen to the sermons for those 15 days and so
then the *circolo Cattolica* was formed and all the girls that is
whoever wanted to, could join, all of my girlfriends because I
had a lot of friends, became members of this catholic
organization and I also joined it was called *gioventu cattolica*,
and we had to go to church every Sunday afternoon and pray, I
never missed it, I would get up early and do everything that had
to be done so that I would be free to go, as I've said when I went
to school I'd been a *piccola Italiana*, and now that I was a
young lady I continued to belong but now we were called
giovane italiane it didn't matter that I had so much to do I
belonged to these organizations just the same, when we had to
do laundry especially during the summer we would go to the
river all us girlfriends we were always 5 or 6 we would prepare a
lot of things to eat and would meet early in the morning, first
we would wash the clothes which took until about 1 in the

afternoon, we would spread the laundry on the grass to dry in the sun and we would eat we would play we would take baths in the river we would sing and it was like going on a picnic and we were happy, we would meet every 15 days during the winter we would go to the fountain but only to wash clothes and it was always like this we didn't have other ways to amuse ourselves there were no cinemas and no one ever went out and never paid attention to any boy, if a girl flirted she was a bad girl, no one ever went out at night, there was no radio or television, as I've said we had vineyards, we made 70-80 quintals of wine a year, and during harvest time there was a lot of work, the women would harvest the grapes and the men, with mules, would take the grapes to Cairano, we had a large cellar, the grapes were brought in with mules because there were no other means but mules to carry them, in the evening other men would crush the grapes, the grapes were crushed by feet in big vats, the men would wash their feet, put short pants on and crush, and all of this work lasted 15 20 days, but it took more than a month to prepare the wine, there was also a lot of work for me to do, I had to go into the field with the other women and bring food for everyone, everyone was happy they would sing grape harvest songs in the evening when everyone returned to Cairano the women farmers would assemble in the street, women who went to sow the wheat, women who went to harvest grapes, and they would sing, laugh, and it was like this also during the harvests for wheat, corn, fava beans, and other harvests, as I've said we had sharecroppers, but during the harvest we had to help a little, every day in the afternoon I would go out to the fields to get the half of the harvest that belonged to us, but then my father did not want to be a shoemaker any longer because the taxes he had to pay didn't leave him with much, and so he gave himself more to the land that is to the vineyards, the wine we made he would sell wholesale to buyers who came from far away, and

some he would sell in the village, our house was in the center of
the village right on the town square it consisted of a large room
on the ground floor on one side where my father had worked but
when he didn't work any longer making shoes he had made a
small kitchen, on the second floor there were 4 rooms, 3
bedrooms and one that was like a sitting room where my father
would gather often with his friends those few *signori* would
come over and play cards, *tre sette scopa* whoever lost would
pay for the wine, they played to pass the time, often they would
just talk my mother would cook for them and I would help her
some friends were hunters and often they would bring birds
rabbits and other animals they would bring fish they had caught
eggs and many other things I remember a certain family that
lived in the country, my mother had been the godmother of two
of their children when they had been baptized, and every Sunday
morning they would come to the village to go to mass and to
buy things, and they had to pass by our house and each time
they would call to my mother and give her a rabbit chicken eggs
cheese they never stopped without bringing something, as I said
we sold wine to the village the cellar was close to our house, and
when people would come to buy wine it usually fell to me to go
to the cellar to get it. there was a poor woman neighbor who
when she would see me go toward the cellar would come with a
big glass and would ask for some wine, I would always give her
some, there was so much of it as you can see, time was passing
and I was growing by now I had learned a decent amount of
sewing and embroidery, my mother told me that I should learn
to knit in order to make sweaters and socks, I did learn how to
make sweaters but I didn't want to learn how to make socks, I
told her that only old ladies made socks, I wanted to learn how
to embroider by machine. my father had bought me a sewing
machine even though I didn't yet know how to use it, he had
had a chance to buy it at half price, I had a school friend who

lived nearby to be honest she was a little vain because she was an only child she was always by herself and never joined our group, she acted as if she were better than us. she had a grandfather in America who sent a lot of money, her father had a brother at Santa Maria Capua near Naples his wife had a machine and knew how to embroider on it they sent her there to learn after 3 months she returned to Cairano she was so happy that she was the only one in the village who knew how to embroider by machine, so I asked her if she would teach me my mother wanted to pay her but she said no she wouldn't teach anyone, I wanted to learn at all costs there was a woman who knew a little but didn't work because she was always sick my mother asked her if she would teach me at first she said no because she didn't feel well but then she took me on I went every day for a week and she would teach me a different stitch every day but then when she had finished showing me what she knew she said that I had to perfect the different stitches on my own, and so whenever I had time I was always at the machine and in a little while I had learned all of the stitches very well, when that friend of mine learned this she got angry and wanted to know who had taught me I didn't tell her because that *signora* had told me not to tell anyone. as I said before, there was no electric light, now a *signore* had come from America who had brought a lot of money and he started making plans to bring electric power to the village since he also owned the mill for the flour which ran on oil which was very dangerous once a woman had died and with electricity it would be better and so after a little while electricity arrived, I remember the day when all the main lines had been installed in the village and they were going to connect the current, that evening all of my father's friends came to our house I have not said that my father was also on the town council they were having a meeting at our house my mother had cooked many things and I had helped and even the mayor was there and he had asked the contractor to please put a temporary line that would bring light inside our house so that they could enjoy themselves better so our house was the first house in the village to have electricity I was so happy, it stayed as it was that first night until the electrician came and put fixtures throughout the house I was 16-17 by now I was a young woman and my mother told me that I had to start making my trousseau for such was the custom, all the young girls had to make a trousseau for themselves, since my mother was sick she was in a hurry for me to make a trousseau she bought the fabric and said that since I had learned to sew and also to embroider I could work on it, there were many boys who were courting me, but I didn't pay attention to any of them it was not yet time, even my parents said it was too early, there was one boy whose parents wanted me and they always came to our house since they were also my father's and mother's friends and spoke of it with them often but my parents told them they would have to wait at least a year I didn't know anything about this the boy would come often with his parents and it was this very one that I married I didn't want anyone around me I liked my situation anyway none of my girlfriends had boyfriends, but my mother was good friends with the mother of this boy, and she didn't want to have to say again that it wasn't time, because they'd already said that before, but he couldn't come to our house more than two times a week, as I already mentioned, I belonged to the *giovane fasciste* and the catholic clubs and all my girlfriends were envious of me they would tell me that I had a boyfriend and I would turn red and get mad at my mother, one night, in 1930 in the month of August I don't remember the date it was close to one in the morning and I was awake and I had the light on because I wanted to see the time because in the morning I had to get up early because my friends and I had to go to the river and do the laundry and I saw that the lamp in the middle of the room was moving and even the paintings on the wall were moving and immediately I started to scream that there was an earthquake I don't know why I said earthquake because I had never seen one before, everyone left their homes, but nothing happened, and for a few nights we left the town out of fright, my sister assunta was 10 years old and she would get scared and each evening she would take her pillow and put it under her arm and cry that she wanted to go away but after 8 days we didn't leave the house any longer, since my father no longer worked as a shoemaker, he and a friend wanted to do something else, so they decided to sell nitrate fertilizers for the land and copper sulfate spray for the vineyards, since everyone had to buy them in other nearby villages, and so there was another job for me, my father had it announced to the village that whoever wanted to buy all the fertilizer they needed had to come and say so, I had to write down their names in a notebook and the quantity they wanted after everyone had come to tell us how much they wanted, my father would send for the amount he needed to the farmer's cooperative at montecatini, and so when the freight train arrived at the station we had to go and get it, and then once again it was announced that whoever had placed an order had to go and pick it up and I had to go with my father, because I had to call all their names and it wasn't a small number more than 1000 quintals, I had to do all of this work because as I've already said my older brother was with the monks, my younger brother was in another town perfecting his trade of cabinetmaking because he had gone to a cabinetmaker in our town, but he had wanted to learn more, my sister was little and so I had to do everything, the housework, go to the country to bring food to the workers who would come to work in the vineyards, go to get half of the harvest from the sharecroppers and when I had time I had to work on preparing my trousseau, I haven't spoken any more about my mother's illness but the

14

more time passed the worse she became, she lost more weight
the doctors couldn't do anything, and the time passed with this
rhythm, I don't remember the year but a disease came to the
vineyards in a short time all the vines became diseased not even
the experts knew what it was but later it was known that it was a
disease called phylloxera there wasn't anything we could do
about it, I remember that when the workers hoed my father lit a
fire and made them pass the hoe through the fire to disinfect it
but nothing was gained by this and in a short time all of the
vineyards were ruined by the disease not only in our village but
in all of Italy and maybe all of Europe, we had a piece of the
vineyard that was isolated actually it was attached to my uncle's
land who also had vineyards, it was not known if there were
other vineyards near those or how it was that these vineyards
held out longer but they did, so my father wanted to plant a
small new vineyard he hired workers to prepare the earth to put
in the new vines but in order to put in new vines we had to buy
american vines, I don't know if they were just called that or if
they really came directly from america, but all of this took a lot
of work and at least 3 years had to pass if all went well to have
the vineyard again and so for this reason we no longer had a lot
of vineyards, and this made me feel bad I even felt like it had
been my fault because when we had had all those vineyards there
was a lot of work to do especially during the harvest and I used
to get mad often I would say that it would be better if all the
vineyards dried up, so there would not be a lot of work, do you
know why, because the harvest was at the end of october and in
the morning I had to go to the river Ofanto and there was
always fog and it was cold my hands almost froze but then the
sun would come out and it would begin to get hot bees would
come because there were a lot of grapes piled up and must
dripping everywhere the bees would bite me and my hands would
swell, this didn't just happen to me but even to the women who

picked the grapes, and so when the vineyards dried up I felt bad and I said that maybe I had made them dry up, but of course that wasn't true because they were sick everywhere, mamma's condition was always worse, she always thought about my brother [Michelangelo] who was far away she wanted to see him, so we sent him a telegram that said our mother was very ill, and he came for 4 days, but when he arrived he began to cry when he saw how worn down she was he said he didn't recognize her any longer, at this point it was almost time for my brother to become a priest, my mother prayed that the Lord would give her the happiness to see her son become a priest before she died, so in the following year he became a priest my parents were very happy they threw a huge feast they invited all of the *signori* in town their friends and all of our relatives cooks came to prepare various dishes there were sweets, liquors and bottled wines that my father had prepared 2 or 3 years earlier this party was in the summer right in the month of June on a Sunday the entire village went to church where my brother and another man were saying their first mass my mother could not walk, but very slowly my father and all the guests brought her I stayed home, how my mother cried, and gave thanks to the lord for having granted her wish, my brother stayed in Cairano a month, each morning he would go and say the mass and even my mother very slowly would go but during this time we spoke of my sister Assunta, my mother who felt that she was near death, said that my brother was now a priest, in a few years I would marry, angelo was also grown, but Assunta was young she was 12 years old, and so my brother wanted her to go to school with the nuns but my sister didn't want to go she said that she didn't want to dress like a nun she didn't like the idea, my brother told her that where he wanted her to go wasn't a convent but an Institute where you studied to become a teacher and they didn't dress like nuns but like a *signorina* and so she said she would go

and so in October of the following year we prepared her
personal trousseau and clothes and she left, almost a year passed
and my mother's condition worsened even more, she'd become
skin and bones and since her blood didn't circulate any longer
her fingers had become deformed and her nerves had constricted
even more then she came down with another illness black dots
on her skin which were very painful, she could not rest each
night she stayed awake and moaned in pain, I who slept in the
room next to hers also stayed awake and prayed to the lord that
he would let her rest and with all of her sufferings she didn't
curse against her destiny, only occasionally did she say lord
maybe I was one of those who put you on the cross, she didn't
want anyone to go out of his way for her, if someone came to
see her, because she could not go out any longer they would say
poor unfortunate woman look what has become of her she
would become mortified she wanted them to tell her happy
things she always had a rosary and was saying the rosary but no
one heard her, I had to help her get dressed and she absolutely
wanted me to get married before she died she was in a hurry for
me to finish my trousseau and so we began the preparation for
my wedding, but she did not see me get married, it was March 3,
1934 a saturday like I said I was part of the *giovane cattoliche*
and during this period we prayed the 15 saturdays for the
madonna of Pompeii and I did them too with my girlfriends, at
nine when I came home from church my mother told me that
she was going to comb her hair and that I had to make her braids
because she couldn't, I always made them for her, when she told
me this, she was speaking well, but after a few minutes she could
no longer speak she became paralyzed immediately we called the
doctor but there was nothing left to do I was alone my brother
Angelo was in the workshop working I called to him my father
had gone to work in the fields to tie the vines we quickly sent
for him but when he arrived she was already dead, she was 53

years old her last words were that she wanted Jesus Christ, that is
the communion, but she didn't make it in time right away
everyone in the village and in the fields knew of her death
because if someone died before noon the bells were rung in
mourning, and since the postman went to the train station at
that time to get the mail everyone in the fields asked him who
had died he said that Filomena Grassi had died those who were
working on our land heard the news, and returned right away to
Cairano they came to our home, in the evening everyone
visited our house funerals lasted 3 days my brother Michelangelo
arrived the day after my mother died and he said the funeral
service. my mother was very well known in the whole village
and everyone came to the funeral, so my mother was gone, the
house was empty, even though she had been very sick but we
still wanted her with us, my brother Angelo always cried he
would go into his room and cry I would tell him that he
shouldn't cry, but he would say that when I got married he would
be left all alone and he thought that our father would remarry he
was 56 years old still young, but he didn't, he showed respect for
my mother he wore black for a long time and if someone told
him to take off his black shirt he responded that if he had been
the one to die my mother would have remained in mourning her
entire life, for more than 6 months he didn't meet with his
friends to play cards like he had done before, he made sure my
trousseau was complete, he thought of all that needed to be done
for my wedding, I had a female cousin who helped him do
everything, after my mother died many things stopped for me,
like the *Gioventu Cattolica* and *fascisti*, I was devastated and
each day that passed I would say that now that my mother was
gone it was useless to continue, now it was getting closer to the
moment I was to be married but I wasn't happy, I didn't want to
leave my house my brother and my father were two men alone,
my brother Michelangelo had returned to the convent, my sister

hadn't come to my mother's funeral, because she wasn't allowed, and so she wouldn't feel bad we hadn't told her anything, she came to know later, so after 10 months the time came that I had to get married but I continued to be devastated because I had lost my mother. I had an aunt who was close to us and to my fiancé's family she took care of everything that I needed, I didn't even want to go buy myself a white dress, I told her how I wanted it I gave her my measurements and they bought it for me, because in my village the bride's wedding dress was bought by the mother of the groom, they would even buy gold jewelry it was all offered as a gift, they bought me the dress and the whole veil, a beautiful necklace a bracelet watch a pin all of 18 karat gold and everything was beautiful, and I liked it. as I've said after my mother's death I no longer belonged to the *gioventu cattolica*, but I wanted to see them one more time, because after I would no longer be a *giovane* but a *donna cattolica*, so during their regular church meeting of the last sunday of the month I brought them wedding favors [*confetti*] and all of them together had bought me a wonderful gift a full set of kitchen pots and pans. and so on January 3, 1935 at ten in the morning I got married my brother married me he came just to marry me and left after a few days my sister didn't come because they did not allow her to come we did not go on a honeymoon because it was not the custom for most, but after a little while we went for a few days to Naples Pompeii so my life changed, before at my house you could say that I did everything the way I wanted, the cooking and all of the housework, I thought about running my house, only my father and my brother Angelo were still there, I went back over to help them, but slowly they adapted they cooked for themselves and I would do their laundry and I felt bad about it, my new life was a little good and a little bad, I had to serve my in-laws because we lived with them because that is how it was done the last son stayed with his parents but I didn't like it everything was different and I had to do everything, my mother-in-law only took care of the cooking the food was different than how we ate at my house and I had to get used to it but I didn't like the situation very much and neither did my husband, when he worked at his trade he had to give the money he earned to his father and when there wasn't work he would go to the fields to work, if I sewed something for someone I had to give the money to my mother-in-law, we never had any money plus I didn't have all those girlfriends any longer, and my husband didn't have any friends either, one day there was a discussion a fight, my father-in-law was mad and said that if we didn't like the situation we should leave, right away my husband left and found a small empty apartment, and that same day we had to leave, I began to cry I didn't like to stay there, but I didn't want to leave either, right away two of my husband's cousins and one of my cousins came and they moved our things there wasn't much anyway only our bedroom set and some other little things, that evening my husband's friends came to see us they were so happy they helped us put our things in place they brought some food and we carried on, my husband was happy because he could do whatever he wanted to do, no longer like a son now he was married and he had the right to anything he wished, to have friends, even I felt better of course we didn't have anything but we were happy the next day we had to prepare something to eat we had only two pots and I remember that that first day we cooked tagliatelle but we had nothing to eat them with one of my husband's cousins lived near our house and he went and asked her for two forks so we could eat them the next day was June 24 there was a fair at Andretta, a nearby town we had a little bit of money, and we went and bought all the utensils that we needed, and so we began our life as a couple, my husband's parents brought us some grain my father brought us other things he felt bad that we had left, but we were happy, we were never alone all of my girlfriends and my husband's friends were always at our house, especially in the evening we played cards and someone would bring something to eat and something to drink, there was one of my cousins Michelangelo who was older than me and he would come every night along with a friend of my husband who also came every night, sometimes they would get embarrassed that they came every evening, and they would tell us to find them girlfriends so that they wouldn't come all the time, often we would all eat dinner together, because there were other male and female friends who would come and someone would bring one thing and someone else another we cooked we ate we laughed and we played a lot of tricks a friend of my husband would help me cook his name was Gerardo and especially when we made ravioli he would tell me that we had to make them all different sizes to make everyone laugh, sometimes in the evenings we were alone, and then all of a sudden friends would come with something to eat and we would make a lot of racket, we were happy, even though we didn't have a lot of course now we had a little piece of land that my father-in-law had given my husband because that was the custom, the father of the groom had to give some land, if he had it, and the father of the bride had to give the dowry, that is money, and the trousseau, of course in both cases they gave whatever they could, depending on their financial situations, and so the children began their own families, and so we also had to go in the fields when there was work to be done, sometimes even our friends would come and help us, and with these same friends we always went to the sanctuaries, to the Madonna delle Puglie to San Michele on Monte Gargano to the fair for San Giovanni to the Madonna dell'Incoronata, but we didn't just go to visit the saints, though there was a lot of devotion in our village, after we did what was necessary in church, we would have a good time, we each brought baskets

with things to eat it was like a little picnic, we had a good time
being all together, I had also renewed my devotion to the
Madonna of Pompeii, once again dedicating 15 Saturdays along
with my girlfriends when I had time I would go to the meetings
with them, I remember that right next to us lived two brothers
Nicola, and Pasquale, so their parents wouldn't know that they
came to our house every night, sometimes they would say that
they were going to bed, but they wouldn't go they would put
blankets and pillows in their beds so that it seemed as if
someone was asleep they would take off their shoes and they
would come with everyone else to our house to play cards,
sometimes these two friends got a good price on vermouth from
some of their relatives and they would bring it and everyone
would put in a little for it, one friend he was the son of a banker
and he always brought a lot of stuff like on the day after Easter
in Italy everyone celebrates it, the day is called *pasquetta*, I
remember he brought a baby goat and he had to kill it himself
but in order to kill it he did all sorts of things to it one could say
he had fun killing it this guy was always joking around, he died
very young in venezuela when we found out we felt very bad his
name was Don Alessio, he was a band leader, but it is pointless
to say more, we were well, when it was necessary to go work in
the fields we went, and when it was necessary we worked in
town, my husband as a cabinetmaker and even I sewed
sometimes with the others, everything was normal we would go
and visit our parents, but all of this didn't last very long, I'm
not sure exactly when but I know that my father-in-law knew
we were happy and that we had a lot of friends, because as I said
our village was small and everyone knew everything he got mad
again about the fact that we didn't want to be with them and we
fought with my in-laws and we were no longer happy like before
our friends still came but we did not carry on like before, on
Christmas eve we were supposed to go to my in-laws' to eat but

I felt bad because my father was alone, but I went anyway but
for me christmas eve was not the way it was supposed to be we
ate and after a while I said that I wanted to go home because I
had a headache, but it wasn't true, my husband could find no
reason to contradict me so we had to leave, soon after we got
home some friends came and they made us a little happier and
so Christmas and the first of the year passed, I have not said
that I was pregnant and in the month of march that is in the
first days of march a baby girl was born she died while she was
being born, all this happened because there was neither a Doctor
nor a midwife during labor, there was only a woman who knew
very little, and when the Doctor came she was dead, I didn't see
her but they told me she was a beautiful girl they gave her the
name of my mother, Filomena, of course I was upset but little
by little it passed but when I would see two of my friends who
had gotten married with me, and they had had two girls it
seemed unfair, and so the two of us were alone, time passed
some good and some bad, we ate from the work in the fields that
is the harvest, and with the work of our trade we bought that
which we needed for the house including supplies, in such a way
we began to get better situated, we always had the same friends,
and went to the same sanctuaries, as was the custom, sometimes
I would go to my husband's parents' fields to help them, but my
father-in-law was always indifferent toward me, sometimes I
would go to my father's house to do something for him, because
now he was really all alone because my brother Angelo had made
a request and been accepted to aviation school, Michelangelo
was with the monks, my sister was at the institute, and when
they would come I would go home to cook, my brother
Michelangelo liked *tagliatelle all'uovo* and a lot of other things
that we made at home, because with the monks he never ate
them, now I was pregnant again and in the month of April,
April 21, 1937 Raffaele was born, this time everything went

well, at this point there was a registered midwife in the village,
and as soon as I felt sick my husband went and called her, this
woman had recently graduated she was a young girl she was from
Venice her name was Ines, she was always chasing young men,
and she could never be found when she was needed, the day
before a woman was having a baby but no one could find her she
was out with some boy and the baby died, so my husband told
her that if she didn't come right away and something bad
happened she would be in real trouble and so she came, she
stayed at our house, I laughed and told her that it was only a
little pain, I was working on two doilies, I worked and she
watched me the baby was born at six in the evening everything
went well the baby was healthy. after 8 days we baptized him his
name like I said, Raffaele comes from the way things were done
in my village if the first child is male he is named after the
father of the father of the baby and my father-in-law was happy
that his name would continue, because his other two sons had
not had any boys and he was even more kind to me, after a little
while the baby became sick, and all of the cures did not help
him, it was not like today that there are lots of nutritious foods
for babies everyone gave children mother's milk and my milk
was very heavy and I couldn't eat anything, but only light
foods, but after a little while he got better and he quickly became
strong so that when he was 3 months old he seemed like he was
6 months old, I had made him a beautiful layette all embroidered
I always dressed him well there were 3 nieces who would come
and get him and take him around all day and everyone admired
him, I had made him a crocheted swaddling band because babies
were swaddled and one time a woman from a nearby village told
me that whoever has pepper puts it even on cabbage, I didn't
understand what those words meant, and she said to me that we
had a lot of money that I had crocheted a swaddling band like
she had never seen before. I told her that we didn't have money

but that it was only my time and a little cotton. the baby grew and we worked and kept going some of our friends got married others were not yet married, but we remained close, some like ourselves who had gotten married also had some land, and we would all work together on each other's land, they would work on our land, and we would work on their land, and so the work was a way to pass the time, especially during the harvest, when we harvested the wheat, we were so happy, after two years that is in 1939 on April 27 I had another baby boy [Peppino], even this time everything went well, but that midwife was no longer there, the town government had sent her away because she never did what she was supposed to do and was always running around as I said earlier, this one was much better she was over 30 from Naples her name was Bianca, now I had 2 babies I had more to do, every two days I had to wash all of their diapers, I had to go to the fountain because as I said earlier there was no water in the village, and while I went to the fountain my husband watched the children, but 4 months later my husband was called to the army for 70 days of training, but in 1940 the second world war started and so my husband did not return, all the men were called to war my husband was already in libya, only women and old men were left. even my brothers were called to war Michelangelo as a chaplain since he was a priest and Angelo in the air force I don't know what he did. now all of our girlfriends and boyfriends had gotten married and so we women were all left alone, but we continued to always be together, we went to work in the fields together one day on each piece, we didn't know how to do a lot of things but little by little we learned, we didn't even understand what was happening in the war, there were no radios, there were no newspapers, we knew a little bit from the few *signori* who bought newspapers from far away, those of us who understood nothing were in the dark the letters that arrived didn't say much, everything had

changed I truthfully like I said didn't know what was happening
in the war, but the government in a short time took all our
copper utensils to make weapons, they took all the gold we had
even our wedding bands, they gave us bronze ones, they took all
the wheat and gave us back 16 kilos of wheat per person, they
gave us a booklet, called the *tessera*, where all that they were
supposed to give us was written, like sugar, oil, salt, and other
things, you could not buy what you wanted not fabric not shoes,
or a lot of other things that you needed, the wheat wasn't
enough for adults especially those who worked hard as farmers,
because when 16 kilos of grain was made into flour, it couldn't
last an entire month, and that was all there was, there was no
pasta, if someone had some grain, then it was not so bad for
them, it wasn't too bad for those who had children, but then
there wasn't enough sugar and so people traded, if you had
children and too much wheat, you would give it away and get
sugar in return, when we had worn out the clothes we had there
was no more fabric to buy, the stores that had some had put it
all aside, and so whoever had enough sheets would dye them to
whatever color they wanted and use them to make clothes,
there was no soap to wash clothes with not even to wash
ourselves, we had learned how to make soap ourselves but you
had to buy a powder I don't remember what it was called you
took some fat and boiled it and when it had cooled it became
soap when we had fat we would make soap. we lacked everything
even matches to start the fire, I remember that next to my
house there was a farming family who always kept a fire going
night and day, I don't know how they did it, every night they'd
put a piece of hard wood under the cinders and that way in the
morning they would always find the fire lit, they were very good
people and every morning they would call me to come and get
the fire, there was a black market if I wanted something from
one of the stores that like I said had put things aside I had to

pay 3 times the cost, it was all like this it's not worth talking about, it was said that in war there were those who died and those who became rich, they would go and stop train cars and ransack them and take all that was on them you couldn't find salt we ate without it and all of this lasted until the very end, when there were bombings everyone stayed home, even the farmers would go to the fields early and come back by ten in the morning, because the sky would be full of airplanes and they'd drop bombs, I remember one day I couldn't find Peppino my younger boy and I found him on the street watching how they were shooting, he really liked how you could see that they were bombing tanks far away and forests were catching on fire, one night I heard a commotion on the street horses passing by, I didn't know what it was but I didn't want to look either, in the morning they told me that at the station they had ransacked a train and had taken everything one of my husband's female cousins and two female neighbors said that even they wanted to go and see if they could take something even I went with them but we didn't find anything, as we were returning the bombing began again and I barely missed being hit by the ricochet of a machine gun bullet. then when the men became prisoners we no longer knew anything, we would go to the red cross to find out something but they never knew anything. we didn't know if they were alive or dead, we even went to women who said they could tell us where they were but they only stole our money, I received a little more than 200 lire a month, I had two children my husband was a sergeant, what could I do with so little money, I had to buy some things for the children, I didn't think about myself, now that they were growing, they needed more, I was alone and I had to go to the fields to work sometimes I would leave them with their grandparents but they didn't want to stay with them my oldest said that his grandfather yelled at them all the time, I'd bring them with me when I had to stay all day, I remember one day in the month of may I had brought them with me and a bad storm came, there was thunder lightning hail, I was scared and even they cried, the field was kind of far from the path that brought you to the village, it was full of water, and so that I wouldn't leave one boy behind as I brought the other one to the road, I put one on my shoulders and the other one in my arms and I brought them to the road when we arrived we were all soaked and I couldn't go on and so it was a rough life, when I had to get workers they were all old, my father would always have to go and see that they worked, I remember once when it was summer, now my children were bigger, and I had to go and pick so many things like beans chick peas and other things and I had to clean the fields after the wheat had been harvested you had to go in the early morning when it was still cool, so in the evening I would tell the boys that in the morning I had to go get wood, I would put bread and cheese on the dresser, and when they woke up they ate but they weren't supposed to go out of the door, because if they went outside there was the bogeyman, I would leave early and along the road I always said the rosary, because even I was scared, and I would return around 10 when I arrived I always found them playing, I did this many times, but maybe the Lord helped me, because nothing bad ever happened, now Raffaele the firstborn was 6 years old and went to school but the second born Peppino was still small, and there was no preschool like during the first world war, when I was small, so I left him with his grandparents, a typhoid epidemic came in the month of November it was contagious Peppino became sick he wasn't well and so I brought my first born Raffaele to my father's so as to not pass it also to him, Peppino was sick for more than twenty days he couldn't eat anything only a little bit of milk, typhoid didn't just hit children because even two adults had it one woman died she had 3 children, and even a young girl who had come from colombia died, in those days doctors didn't understand many diseases, there was no medicine, not even milk, everyone who had sick people in their families would pay a man and would send him to a nearby village where there were those who kept cows, and you had to mix half water and half milk, I remember that when we couldn't have any milk, we would make it with almonds, we'd clean them mash them in a mortar put them in water filtered them and then drink it, but my son would still be hungry, I never let him see me eat and I would tell him there was no food, this lasted as I said 20 days, I remember that it was Christmas day and the boy could eat a little bit of semolina, but a few days after the younger one was feeling better, the older one got sick even though I had kept him away from home, he got sick anyway but not as bad as his brother, imagine how tired I was, and all this time I stayed alone for fear that someone who didn't have it would also get it, but then it passed, and out of all of those who had had it because there had been a lot only 2 died but like I said they were adults. I have forgotten to say what we ate not only during the war but always we made barley for the children it was like wheat everyone grew it and roasted it we ground it and it was cooked like coffee it seemed just like coffee if you had milk then you put half milk and half barley you added sugar and pieces of bread and gave it to all the children young and older in the morning, sometimes we cooked bread with oil and garlic and you'd give them that, and sometimes we gave them pastina that had also been cooked with oil and garlic, all of these things were all better than all of these sweet things of today, because these were all natural there was no caffeine in barley, at midday there was bread with something, and in the evening we cooked soups, we used many starches often pasta but made by hand, not bought, we ate it almost every day we made different types as I said in the beginning like my mother had taught me. I haven't said anything else about my husband in the war like I said before we didn't know anything, I'm not good at explaining everything, but he was taken prisoner and then we knew nothing else we turned to the red cross, and to others but after 7 months we only knew he was a prisoner, one day I received a letter it was all erased, I couldn't understand a word and it was explained to me that whatever was written was not good and that's why it had been erased, but now at least we knew he was alive, after a little while I received a letter that he had written from the U.S.,[2] I didn't understand, I asked if he is a prisoner how can the letter come from America I don't remember from where, I went to a neighbor who had come from America and he told me that my husband was a prisoner in America that I could be happy because the war was over for him he got a map of the U.S. and he showed me but as I said I don't remember where I seem to remember that he was taken prisoner in 1942 and all this time he had been first in England and then like I said in America, now I had news from him more often but only a few words that he

---

[2]Ruberto's husband was taken prisoner in Libya by the British. Throughout the rest of his life, he used to tell his family about the tour of the world he was taken on as a prisoner of war, recalling, for instance, how beautiful Durban, South Africa was, and that there were a lot of wild rabbits in Australia.

It is hard to say where he was taken exactly, but we do know that the British eventually turned some of their prisoners, including Ruberto's husband, over to the U.S. We also can say for certain that at some point he was taken to England and then to the United States. In the U.S. he spent time in the states of New York, Ohio, Missouri, and finally California. When he was at Camp Clark in Missouri, he was visited by his brother, Pietro, who had emigrated to the U.S. before the war and was living in Pittsburgh, Pennsylvania. During that trip to Missouri, Pietro also stopped to visit his own son, Fortunato, who was a U.S. Aviation Cadet at Maxwell Field in Alabama (see *The Pittsburgh Post Gazette*, Second News Section, July 3, 1943). By the time he was brought to the Benicia Arsenal in California, he was part of an Italian Service Unit, no longer, strictly speaking, a prisoner of war (see "The Long Journey Back to Italy/Former POW Returns to Benicia," by Bob Silva, *Benicia Herald*, May 29, 1985).

was well. even my brother Angelo was taken prisoner and we had no news from him either, we only knew where the chaplain [Michelangelo] was, but not what he was doing I can only explain that he helped all the people who escaped during bombings he wanted to bring them to the convent especially the children but the brothers didn't want that because they said they had no room, so my brother would help them however he could and with his salary he helped these poor refugees. in the village we continued with the same life, Peppino got sick again he was very sick he had bronchitis and pneumonia and it was very serious, the doctor said that if his high fever did not go down, there would be nothing to do, but after 4 days he got better, during this period my father-in-law died without seeing his son return it was February 27, 1943, I was only at the funeral a short time, because it lasted 3 days, because Peppino was still sick, and then my mother-in-law was left alone she often came to our house and she wanted us to come and live with her since I had to pay rent where we lived but I said we would come when the year that I had paid was over, and so in the month of October we went to live with her, we stayed together for a little while but I didn't like it much, the house was big so we split it, we made two rooms for her, and 3 for me, we were near and we helped each other, and so we kept going until the very end of the war. when the allies came the americans because Italy had lost they sent us many things to eat and to wear and we were a little better off, I remember that when my brother the chaplain came to the village he brought a lot of things because he was in charge of distributing the things that came from america, the war ended in 1945, I was at home that day and I heard a lot of noise outside everyone was screaming and I went outside and they told me that the war was over but Italy as I said had lost I don't remember exactly but it was at the end of August September, but the scare was over no more young people would

31

die, it was said that soon the prisoners would come home, and my husband was one of the first ones to return to my village it was October 5 he said he hadn't been well, and so they sent him home right away he had made the trip from Lioni a village kind of far from us on foot there was no other means of travel because all the bridges of the roads and railways had fallen with the bombs and so he arrived at 2 in the morning, when I heard someone knock at the door I got scared when I saw that it was him, I couldn't believe it he was in fairly good condition out of all the young men of the village who had left I don't remember but I think that 3, 4 died they called them missing but they never returned, the prisoners returned one after another and so it ended, Italy had been destroyed. if we couldn't live before the war, imagine after, there was a little bit that came from america and we carried on. like I said my brother the chaplain helped the refugees during the war and he gave all of his salary to them, after the war when he returned to the convent his superiors wanted all of the money that he had earned during the war my brother told them that he didn't have any that he had given it to the refugees, and so they told him that there was no longer a place for him, and so my brother was no longer a monk but a layman and so he went to Rome and began doing something since he had three degrees, even my sister was sent away from the institute she was at because it was run by the dominicans where my brother had been and she also stayed in Rome my brother Angelo came to the village he had been a prisoner in Germany. after a little while my husband began to work again in his trade as a cabinetmaker but there was no work, we had two boys now both were big and went to school we lived tranquilly it didn't matter that we had nothing, with the fields we could eat, but on July 31, 1946, a baby girl was born we gave her the name Beatrice my husband had read the divine comedy and he liked Beatrice so that his mother wouldn't be upset when she was baptized we gave her the name Beatrice Ernestina like his mother, she was a beautiful baby girl and everyone who knew us, that is our friends the wives who came to visit asked me where we had found that beautiful name, Beatrice and in her crib she seemed like an angel, but she cried often and each evening for 8 days Bianca the midwife came and put her in water and so she didn't cry so much, but this time I wasn't able to make the little layette like I had done for the first two children, because there wasn't anything to buy because of the war, a relative of my sister-in-law who was in America, I didn't know her but my husband did, sent me a nice package full of linen for children, there were many beautiful things inside that no one had ever seen before in my village, even my husband's sister sent me a package, now almost everyone who had someone in America had packages, because there was nothing left in Italy because of the war, now we had 3 children but life was hard there was no work and the days passed a little bad and a little good but in 1948 on November 16 another baby girl was born I remember that one of my husband's nieces had made a list of names for us to call her but I said that we would call her Ernestina like my mother-in-law, but my mother-in-law wanted us to call her after my dead mother, and so when she was baptized they gave her the name Ernestina Maria Filomena, Maria Filomena remained only in the baptismal papers that was the custom and so only Ernestina remained, and so we had four children the first Raffaele like my father-in-law, the second Peppino like my father, Beatrice and Ernestina like my mother-in-law and mother, now my husband wanted to go somewhere to work because in Italy there was nowhere for him to go, he didn't know anyone, people started to talk about Venezuela, but they said that it wasn't a nice place, that the climate was too hot and the people were bad it was said that they lived like savages that everything was different from us but it was also said to give it a try, there was a distant nephew of my husband's who was a plumber, he couldn't find any work he had two children and you could say that he was desperate, and he wanted to go to Venezuela, but everyone advised him not to go but he wanted to go and then he sent word to say that it wasn't so bad and then another two went and so my husband went too he prepared the papers and left it was the month of July 1949 he left me with 4 children, now I was alone and I had to do everything like when there had been the war, I had to work in the fields, and I had to take care of 4 children not two, but there was my mother-in-law who watched them when I went to the fields, since she was nearby and sometimes I brought the girls with me, the boys went to school, others left for Venezuela they were all our friends, we wives did the same things as before one day we went to work in one place the next in another and we stayed together and helped each other, but not everyone who went to Venezuela made a fortune, and so my husband was one of these, he couldn't find work, just enough to support himself, and he waited for things to get better and he sent a little money to us, and so it was always the same I had 4 children the boys went to school and they always had to be clean, we didn't have a lot of clothes and so that they would always be clean and well put together, I would wash in the evening, and in the morning I ironed and they went to school clean but then Raffaele finished elementary school because as I said in the beginning there were only 4 grades, my brother and sister lived in Rome and I sent him to them so he began the upper grades and he stayed with them and I sent money when I could and they kept him there to study, and during the vacations all 3 would come to the village, but it was a sacrifice, then even Peppino finished school, but I couldn't send him to Rome because they had no room, and he did the 5th grade privately, he passed and they advised me to have him also do the middle school grades privately, there was a teacher who had also been my friend, she was my age and we had gotten married in the same year, I asked her to prepare him to take the exams in Rome, the boy was very intelligent, he did so well that in one year he passed two grades. Peppino stayed in Rome only for a short time he said that if his father went to the united states he also wanted to come to america. now even my brother Angelo was in Rome with the air force, he had met a girl from Verona while he was in the war, during the war girls could write or send things to soldiers, this girl's name was Renata and she had written and sent him some packages, when the war was over, he searched for her, they fell in love and got married he had a position in Rome so they were all in Rome my brother Michelangelo now that he was no longer a monk had a position in the department of internal affairs, and they [Internal Affairs] had built apartment buildings, and whoever had a family could have one, I don't know how he got one, but he gave it to his brother who had a family, my husband wasn't having any luck in Venezuela, and in addition the Venezuelan government said that all the foreigners who were working there had to either call for their families or go away, because no more money could leave the country, because now there were a lot of foreigners there almost all Italians. my husband had made a request to go to North America and he had to wait, he had written me and told me that I had to leave the boys in Italy, and go to him with the two girls, he had to claim us as his wife and children, but I didn't want to go, because first of all I didn't want to leave the boys and also where would I go with two young girls when the climate wasn't good for them, and then if he didn't work how could we live I told him that if he went to the U.S. I would come and so after a long time his turn came, he didn't write me from Venezuela to tell me that he was to go but he wrote me from

N.Y. saying that he had arrived in the United States he was at his brother Alessio's[3], he wrote us on December 18, 1953, we received the letter after 3 days it was two days before Christmas[4] I was so worried because it had been a while since I had had any news and when the letter arrived we were all happy especially Peppino who didn't want to go to Rome anymore but wanted to go to America. after the holidays he went to Pgh.[5] where he had his sister other brother and his brother-in-law, who was also a cabinetmaker, so he helped him find work he went to work with him, and lived with them, he began to prepare the papers for us, I wasn't too happy because I had to leave my family, and especially my father and mother-in-law who were old, even they felt bad that I had to leave, but I had promised and I had to come, I have forgotten to say that the year before my sister-in-law and her husband, that is my husband's sister, had come to Italy and had seen the life I lived every day in the fields, how the boys and the young girls lived and what we ate they knew that my husband had made a request to go to N.A. they told me that if he succeeded I had to without a doubt come to America and not do as I had done before by not going to Venezuela, I remember that even my brother Angelo told me, they all felt bad that I was going away but I had to do it, because in Italy with 4 children I couldn't give them a future, the problem was that Raffaele was studying he was in high school and he wanted to stay at least to finish high school, and so he stayed I prepared all of our documents as soon as we received the permission to emigrate, I gave the land to someone who would work it, the house remained with my mother-in-law since

---

[3] Alessio moved back and forth between Italy and the U.S. before and after the war. After WWII he was living in the Bronx.
[4] The time sequence is equally unclear in the original.
[5] She uses the local abbreviation "Pgh." for Pittsburgh, Pennsylvania. He moved to Bloomfield, the Italian American neighborhood of Pittsburgh.

it was hers, I sold or gave away the little supplies we had, I sold the harvest, I worked a lot to do all of this but there was Peppino who willingly helped me, all of the women I knew were sad that I was leaving, two of my friends had gone to Venezuela, and one had also left for America, because even her husband had been in Venezuela and had gotten a visa before my husband's, and so only a few of my girlfriends were left, all the women I sewed clothes for felt bad, and I won't even tell you how sad my sister felt, when she would come during vacations she would always stay at home, and sometimes she would even come to the fields to be with me, and so after I had prepared everything I could bring, I put it all in trunks, because we were going by boat, we could bring a lot of things, and so we left on November 30, 1954, when we said goodbye to my father he was crying and he said that I shouldn't leave him, because I was the only one of his children who had stayed a long time with him, even my mother-in-law was crying, but I could do nothing, I had to obey my husband because even he was right, he had always been alone in the world, 7 years in the war and as a prisoner, and 4 years in Venezuela, I remember that when we got into the car to leave there were a lot of people around us, one of my brothers stayed behind with my father and one came with us, and my sister came from Rome to Naples to say goodbye to us, it was the last goodbye because I never saw anyone again, we stayed in Naples for two days to pass all of the medical exams and so we left leaving Italy and all of my dear ones especially my son Raffaele with the hope that he would meet us soon, the voyage was bad for Beatrice and me especially Beatrice, in the 10 days that the trip lasted she never ate not even a glass of milk, one of the waiters who served us because we were in first class told me to force her to eat something or else she wouldn't make it to America, the trip went well for Peppino and Ernestina, the sea didn't make them sick, after 10 days we arrived in N.Y. where my husband and his brother were waiting for us, of course N.Y. looked like a paradise to us, when we heard people talking we didn't understand anything, we stayed in N.Y. 3 days and then we left for Pgh. all day on the train, when we arrived at the station in Pgh. my brother-in-law was there waiting for us, when we arrived at the house there was my sister-in-law and all of her children, I knew her because she had come to Italy the year before. my husband had bought a little house[6] it wasn't very nice but while he had been waiting for us he had fixed it up, everyone had given him something and we found everything ready, of course it wasn't much but enough to start and we continued to work on it and finished fixing it up, like I said it wasn't very nice, but it was always better and with more comforts than what we had left, it had water, and gas, which in the village we had not had, actually when we left they were putting in the lines to bring water to the village, and so a new life began for us, right away the girls went to school and even Peppino went. Beatrice was 8 years old and had passed 3rd grade in the village and they put her in second grade and Ernestina hadn't begun, because she was 6 years old so they put her in first grade, Peppino went to 8th grade since he had already finished middle school but he quickly passed to high school, my husband went to work and I stayed home, because I couldn't work outside of the home since I didn't speak the language, of course it was difficult for me when I went to do the shopping I never went alone at first, but then everything became easier because there were almost all Italians in the neighborhood where we lived they spoke Italian even in the stores I began to get to know people who had come from Italy before us. and then people say that it's easy to pass from bad to good, but you don't get used to going from good to bad, but us having come from the bad, we were much better off, but I

---

[6]The house was on Juniper Street in Bloomfield.

often thought about my family who had remained in Italy, especially my son and the old people, we sent some money to my brothers for Raffaele, but my husband didn't work all of the time, he didn't work more than six months out of the year[7] he didn't work in the winter they gave us a little unemployment money but there were 5 of us, and sometimes it didn't last to the next week, and so Peppino didn't want to go to school any longer he wanted to learn to be a barber, he had to go to barber school for 5 months and then he also went out to look for work and he helped a little with his job, because in those first days we were not too well off but we were always better than we had been we could eat more, and the girls could drink as much milk as they wanted, because in the village they had it only when they were sick, from Italy we got news that everyone was well and that Raffaele was doing well in school, almost 3 years had passed and he still hadn't been called for the physical exam needed for him to come to America, we were a little worried because if he turned 21 he would no longer be able to come, we knew a *signora* a neighbor whose brother was a congressman in Wascinton [Washington] and this *signora* wrote a letter to him to see if he could do something, and this man was so kind he responded telling us not to worry that before he turned 21 he would come, and so it was, he came before he turned 21 now especially for me thoughts of Italy had diminished a little, like I said while we were waiting for Raffaele who was supposed to come to America our house was small we wanted to buy another bigger one of course we didn't have the money you had to pay monthly but a down payment was needed and so my husband's brother loaned us 2 thousand dollars and we bought a larger

---

[7]He worked in the local carpenter's union and was usually unemployed during the winter months as there was very little outdoor work, and sometimes he found only indoor work.

house[8] it had 4 bedrooms and it was in a better area and so we bought it in the month of march in april we cleaned it and went to live there we went with the idea that my husband would be in good health and that he would have work but misfortune came and in the month of november actually on the eve of the holiday my husband got hurt while working they were making a large garage he was in the ditch and was putting up the wood forms when dirt fell on top of him and the hole began to cave in it was November 27, 1957, imagine how scared I was I couldn't go right away the contractor who called me told me not to worry that it wasn't bad but he said that not to scare me Peppino was at work and I didn't have his telephone number I called my sister-in-law but they couldn't do anything they had to come in the evening they brought him to the hospital it was far and when it was evening I left the girls at a neighbor's and Peppino and I went. when we arrived he was all bandaged and he had scratches on his face imagine if something really serious had happened how would I have managed with a newly bought house and 4 children I knew nothing of this land, but I only had to thank the Lord that it had come out like this little by little he got better he went from that hospital to another one nearer his boss paid me weekly as if he had been working because it had been the boss's fault and 6 months passed before he could work again. during this time as I said Peppino had learned to be a barber and he was working he had met a girl whose family came from Italy she was a good girl and they wanted to get married we didn't find anything to object to only that they were very young but they loved each other, and so they were married. but after a little while my sister wrote that my brother Angelo wasn't doing too well, he had a stomach ulcer, they had to operate, they operated it seemed as if all had gone well, he

---

[8] The house was on South Evaline Street in Bloomfield.

continued to have pains in his stomach he was operated again he
had the incurable illness, there was nothing that could cure him
and after 3 months of atrocious suffering on October 14, 1958,
he died he was 43 years old and he left behind a 6 year old
daughter, the pain for me was great and I still remember his
words, when he said who knows if we would see each other again,
he was one of the members of my family who died young
without me seeing him again when he had been sick he wrote me
with his own hands he asked if we could help him if we could
find better medicine here, my husband went to the doctor but he
said that with that illness there was nothing you could do, we
sent 100 dollars to my unfortunate brother but it arrived after
he had died, the way his letter had been written made me cry,
maybe you don't believe me but I kept it a long time and every
once in a while I would read it. of course for all of them his
death had been more painful than for me because they saw him
suffer, my brother Michelangelo was never the same after the
death of his brother all of Angelo's sufferings had remained in
his head and when he wrote me he said he always thought of
him, they didn't tell my father anything of his illness he learned
after they wanted him to remember Angelo always in good
health like when he used to go to the village, he would wake up
early and go to the fields to look at everything, and when he
returned he would always bring fresh fruit, he was always so
happy that he had had such a nice walk, but he felt sick all the
same, but he wanted to see everything all the same. here
Raffaele had gone back to studying he went to the university in
the evening and during the day he worked in a laboratory in the
same university, he had a fiancée in Italy and as soon as he had
made a little money he would go back and marry her and so it
happened, but while he was in Italy he was called to the military
and after a month he returned to America and his wife stayed in
Italy with her parents. in the month of May he left for the

army he stayed in Georgia for 3 months and then they sent him to Germany[9], after a little while his wife met him there and they stayed for two years, during this time he asked for permission for his wife to come to America, and when he was discharged from the service they came together. the years were passing, my father was always at the village, he didn't like to be in Rome he was used to his house, used to his village, he had a lot of friends, he didn't want to leave his way of life, and every once in a while my brother and sister went to see him, they had gotten a woman who helped do his housework, but he was always a worry for them, and so on November 22, 1964, he died he was not sick he died in his sleep like he had always said he would, he prayed to the Lord to let him die quickly, he was 86 years old, he had never been sick, he only suffered from a little arthritis the evening before his death he had been with his friends, when I learned of his death, it was more pain for me, never to see him again, because we couldn't go to Italy with the little money we had, one needed only to be resigned to that fact, I made myself feel better thinking that he hadn't been sick because being far away I would not have even been able to give him a glass of water, he had done so much for me, and I had done nothing for him, now only my brother Michelangelo, and my sister Assunta, and my sister-in-law with the little girl were left, they all felt bad, but life had to continue, each did his own work, my sister-in-law and the girl lived in the house that as I said earlier my brother had transferred to them and the other two stayed in an apartment together, but they were not there a long time, because another misfortune came, it was May 3, 1965, my brother fell as he was going to the office to work, he had a heart attack and died as they were bringing him to the hospital. after

---

[9] He was stationed at the Mansfield Kaserne, the U.S. military base in Straubing on the Danube, West Germany.

8 days my son Raffaele who as I said was married and now had his own house and already had a baby boy, came to the house to give me the bad news, he didn't know how to say it, because barely 7 months had passed since my father had died, he began to cry and I understood right away that there was more bad news, he told me that Michelangelo was gone, that he had died of a heart attack, I couldn't believe it, it was so sad, only two days earlier I had received a letter where he had told me to watch out for my own health since I have high blood pressure, he told me to be careful of what I ate, he said that he was well and that his blood pressure was more low than high, even this last letter from him I kept like the one from my other brother, even he had gone young, he was 55 years old now only Assunta was left, here everything continued a little good and a little bad the boys were married had children and worked I have not told you that Raffaele stayed in germany for two years and when he returned he finished school and got a degree in chemistry and got a job with golfo [Gulf Oil] where he works still and Peppino always worked as a barber and they are well off, the girls were now in high school. during this time period even my mother-in-law died she was old she was 95 she died of old age and I felt bad one of her sons [Pietro] had returned to Italy and had been with her but let us say that when someone dies old there is little that is bad because we know that they must die, my husband felt well with all that had happened to him, of course he always felt some pain, like always he only worked 6 months out of the year, I stay home my health is not bad, I am under the care of a doctor to control my blood pressure, I stay home I do everything like my mother taught me, I cook I make bread, make pasta by hand, and sew some things for myself, I have never bought myself a dress, I make them for myself I crochet I knit, I work in the yard, cut the grass, grow flowers, and have a vegetable garden, because we have a lot of land around our house

we grow tomatoes peppers greens and beans and I can them all
for winter, and so the days pass, my sister and I write to each
other, of course she's alone. she works she says she's well, she
thinks she would like to buy an apartment because homes are a
little scarce in Rome and the rent is high, she says that the
landlord where she was living was old and wants to sell, after a
little while, in the month of September, she wrote to tell us she
had bought it, she put a little money down and the rest she
would pay monthly, but she was unlucky, after 2 months while
she was in a conference at work she didn't feel well right away
they brought her to the hospital she had had a stroke she was in
the hospital for 20 days but then on November 13, 1969, she
died, she had had a cerebral thrombosis, when my son received
the news, since his wife's parents lived in Rome they would
always write to him, so he came to our house he didn't know
how to tell me but I understood that he had to tell me
something bad, I started to cry my family was gone I no longer
had anyone everyone was dead even my young sister she was 49
years old, in 10 years my family had all died, I no longer had the
will to do anything I always thought about them, and I would say
that soon I would also have to go, but very slowly I resigned
myself to my situation my sister-in-law and my niece were
alone, after a while my husband went to Italy to see things,
because as I have said we had land outside of the village, there
was the house that my sister had bought, poor woman she
hadn't even had the time to fix it up, now it had to be resold to
pay the debt that had been made to buy it, I didn't want to go
they were all dead and I didn't feel like going I made my husband
my proxy and he went to try and do something, along with my
sister-in-law, because she who represented her daughter was an
heir, I had remained but I felt dead along with them, and I
thought about all the good they had all done for me. when they
had kept my children especially Raffaele who had stayed with

them until he had come to America, and even he remembers
them always. in 1971 I had a desire to see some of my family,
but I didn't want to go to Italy, I had a cousin from both my
mother's and father's side of the family, because my mother
and her mother were sisters and had married two brothers we
were real cousins of the same blood this cousin was in Venezuela
and I told my husband that I wanted to go and see her at least
for 8 days and so we went, poor woman, even she had a husband
who wasn't well, he had diabetes, he had a little sore on his foot
that would not heal it was said that with diabetes it would never
heal, but then in 1972 in the month of April after much
suffering he died from that sore cancer developed and he died he
was also young and he had 2 children, my husband was very
moved and shocked by this, this man had been one of his friends
he was actually one of those young men as I said before who
would pretend to sleep and come to our house in the evening,
and so my husband said that he wanted to go to Italy and that I
had to go also, he said that if we didn't go now we would never
go again, I made him happy and we went in the month of May
1973, my sister-in-law was waiting for us, none of my brothers
or sister were there not my parents and not even those of my
husband, the day after we arrived in Rome we went to the
cemetery right away to bring flowers, how upsetting it was to
see their photos on their graves all so young, especially my
brother Michelangelo, with that smile, because he was always
laughing and when we would get mad he used to tell all of us not
to get mad, because life is short, as if he knew that he was to die
young, and then we went to the village and even here we went
to the cemetery to see the tombs of our parents before anything
else, we stayed in Italy 45 days always traveling to see the
sanctuaries those that we had been to when we were young, we
went to Milan Venice Pisa Florence Rome Naples Pompeii
Capri Sorrento Salerno Avellino we passed through a lot of

villages and stayed at some like Caposele and Materdomini, we stayed there for 3 days there was a big sanctuary San Gerardo Maiella it's very famous in those parts and it's near our village we also went through Puglia Foggia on Monte Gargano, we only stayed a little in our village, our friends weren't there any longer there were some cousins but everyone had gone away some abroad and some to northern Italy to work. almost everyone had gone to Turin so we went to Turin almost just to see them, I had two close cousins and their families there and we had some friends from our youth there, and in Turin I felt a little bit like I was back with my family we stayed 8 days in Rome we stayed with my sister-in-law I felt awful that none of my brothers or my sister were there we stayed 2 days with the parents of my daughter-in-law Anna, they had come to America to see their daughter and we had met them and after 45 days we returned to America, I didn't cry when I left Italy to return to America since I wasn't leaving anyone, actually it seemed like a million years before I could return home to see all of my children my husband began to work again, but he worked only a short time one or two years, because he no longer felt like working he was 62 years old and he retired, I remained like before doing all of the housework, but now that my husband no longer worked he busied himself with the yard cutting the grass and other things but I planted the vegetable garden because he didn't know how to do a lot of things, time passed like always, the two girls now had grown they were still in school at the university, the two sons had their own families at their own houses, now even I was 62 years old and even I got a pension, of course it was what I received for my husband's work because I had never worked anywhere, my health is no longer like it used to be I don't know if I said that I have high blood pressure but now I also have asthma I can no longer breathe well I've been to the hospital 4 times, but this illness doesn't pass, you live on only with medicine, but when I'm fairly well I do everything like always, my husband tells me that I never stay still, and I respond that whoever stays still is dead and I continue, sometimes I get mad at him because he doesn't do anything, and he could do more, he likes to read a lot and he does that, but now the 2 of us are left alone the girls now that they have finished school have gone to work in New York on Long Island they haven't married, the two sons aren't in the city like we are but they have bought themselves houses outside of the city but they aren't far and we see each other every week, they are well and they each have 3 children, the older has two girls and a boy, the younger has 3 girls even my sister-in-law died last year no one is left any longer my niece got married, but she has always been indifferent toward us, we have always mailed her things we gave her a nice present when she got married we don't write each other often, in 1980, on November 23 there was an earthquake in Italy right around our parts that is in the province of Avellino where my village is 50 percent of my village was damaged, we were very upset but fortunately there were no victims, but my husband always wanted to see how it was damaged, and this year he could no longer resist his desire to see our village, and so he decided to go, I couldn't go because as I said I have asthma which bothers me a lot, and then I no longer have anyone, I would have to go again to see their tombs I would have even gone but with my health I can't, it's better to remember my village the way I left it 28 years ago, beautiful clean high on a hill 815 meters above sea level with air clean and fresh and on one side of the village in the morning one could see the sunrise and in the evening the sunset with the sun going down with such rays of fire, and at night the moon with the stars that shined were so clear that we used to count them when we were children, it is now 28 years that I find myself here in America I've never been able to see the sky blue with the sun that shines clean and I've never seen the night so beautiful with the clear moon and the stars, in the spring the swallows would come from the warm places by the thousands to make things better with their song as if they wanted to say we have arrived, and in autumn by themselves they would line up on the electric lines to then leave again for warmer places because winter came to us, my village was poor but beautiful, don't you think that I was happy to leave it, I'd lived there until I was 43 years old, but I wanted to leave for my children, and so now my husband has gone to see it in the company of my daughter Beatrice I find myself here on Long Island with my other daughter Ernestina I like to stay here and to stay with her is right, but I miss one thing it seems that here the days are all the same there is never a Sunday, for me Sunday means that I have to go to mass, I'm used to that and for me it seems that if on a Sunday I don't go to church I haven't done everything, something is missing, I remember that when we were children, if sometimes we didn't feel like going, my mother would tell us whoever doesn't go to mass doesn't eat, the village was so religious I remember those that lived in the countryside during the cold and the snow they would come each Sunday to mass, here I don't go to church it's far, the world has changed, the people of today have put faith aside, people think only of hurting killing stealing there's no shame, you could say that the animals are more correct, who knows if maybe God is punishing us for people's bad behavior. when God created the world he made it beautiful, but we who live here have made it ugly, my story is over. this which I've said from the beginning is all true, there are a lot of things that with my mind I remember but I don't know how to write, because I don't have the education, 60 years ago I finished the fourth grade in a little village like I said in the beginning with my sick mother, now in three months I'll be 70 years old, I've worked a lot and have had many displeasures, but I'm still on this earth, my destiny was not like

that of my brothers or of my sister who all left young or like
my mother also who was 53, and had suffered a lot, tomorrow if
God is willing my husband will arrive from Italy with my
daughter and they will tell me everything, but it is better not to
know. in 8 days we will return to Pgh. where my other children
and grandchildren are waiting for me and even my cat, poor
thing he was always with me who knows how he searches for me
now, I will begin my habits again, to clean the house be in the
yard mass on Sunday, and a lot of other things, only I'm sad to
leave my daughters again far away, but such is life. even I left
my father and all my dear ones never to see them again.

Ma la vita è fatta così

mio marito si rimise a lavorare, ma lavorò poco tempo uno o 2 anni, perchè non si sentiva più di lavorar, aveva 62 anni e andò in pensione, io lo stesso come prima con (tutte le faccende di casa, ma adesso che mio marito non lavorava più si interessò lui in giardino a togliere l'erba e altri lavori ma nell'orto lo aiutavo io di tante cose non le sapeva fare, il tempo scorreva come sempre, le due ragazze ormai grandi andavano ancora a scuola le ~~pro~~ in università i due figli avevano le loro famiglie ~~Raffaela e figli~~ e tutti alle loro cose, adesso anch'io aveva 62 anni e anch'io aveva la pensione, certo era quella che mi aspettava dal lavoro che aveva fatto mio marito perchè io non avevo lavorato in nessun posto, ~~adesso~~ ~~~~ * continuo il N 5 ora adesso ~~andiamo~~ siamo rimasti solo noi due, le ragazze finiti le scuole se ne sono andate per lavoro sono andato in in N.Y. in long Island ~~e ho~~ non si sono ~~~~ ~~~~ sposate, continuo il N 4 ~~figli~~, stanno bene anche 3 figli ciascuno, il primo a 2 femmine e un maschio

Ma la vita è fatta così

Leonilde Frieri Ruberto

il mio paese era piccolo 1500 abitanti, si chiamava Cairano
prov. Avellino, cittadini, contadini tutti lavoravano la terra di
loro proprietà, anche i cittadini pur avendo il mestiero
coltivavano la loro terra, i contadini quando andavano alla
loro terra a lavorare, e quando andavano a lavorare dai
cittadini per guadagnare un po' di soldi per le spese che
avevano per loro, vi erano pochi signori ricchi di terra che
avevano i coloni, io sono nata il 2 gennaio 1913, mio padre
era calzolaio mia madre era casalinga, aveva un fratello due
anni più di me, cerano i nonni, il padre di mia madre era solo
la nonna era morta prima che io nasciessi, e i vecchi non si
facevano stare soli, mia madre aveva 4 sorelle e così mio
nonno stava 4 mesi per parte dalle sue figlie, che con mia
madre erano 5, il nonno era aiutante al municipio portava alla
gente tutte le carte delle tasse, il municipio li mandava a mano
le tasse non per posta, mio padre aveva tutte e due nonna e
nonno, ma poi morì la nonna, e così anche il nonno di mio
padre dovettero fare la stessa cosa, mio padre aveva altre due
fratelli e si tennero un po' per uno il loro padre, quando stava
a casa ci raccontava sempre storielle, di fantasmi, come
venuto al mondo Gesu cristo, non lavorava piu era vecchio,
prima lavorava le sue terra, queste terre se le divisero tutte e
tre i figli il 23 marzo 1915 naque mio fratello Angelo io
avevo poco piu di due anni, e nel mese di maggio il 24 scoppiò
la prima guerra, poco dopo anche mio padre fu richiamato in
guerra, la guerra durò tre anni, io incominciavo a capire
qualche cosa mi ricordo che a 3 anni andavo alla scuola dei
piccoli dalle suore, tutti i figli dei richiamati mangiavano alla
mensa governativa e giocavamo andavo solo io e mio fratello

Michelangelo, ma Angelo era troppo piccolo e non poteva
venire, mia madre durante la guerra lavorava tanto, aveva 3
figli i nonni quando uno e quando l'altro poi cera la campagna,
mi ho dimenticato di dire che mio padre oltre a essere
calzolaio cerano anche delle terre e dei vigneti, la terra la
lavoravano i coloni ma le vigne la lavoravano un po' loro, e
mettevano i contadini a fare i lavori pesanti, tutto queste
doveva fare mia madre con qualche donna a giornata, perche
gli uomini erano tutti in guerra, e cosi anchio facevo qualche
cosa, mia madre mi portava con se in campagna quando
andava, io cullava mio fratello piccolo lo guardavo che non si
faceva male e così mia madre come ho detto che lavorava
tanto a poco a poco le sue forze non ce la facevano a fare
tanto lavoro e non si sentiva tanto bene con la salute, ma
non se ne curava tirava avanti, aveva una sorella piu grande di
lei zia Colomba la aiutava tanto, perche suo marito non era
andato in guerra perché era vecchio, ci volevo tanto bene loro
non avevano figli, durante la guerra mia madre non cucinava
mai ci faceva mangiare sempre pane e qualche altra cosa,
perché mio padre era in guerra, zia Colomba ci portava
sempre qualche cosa, loro allevavano piccioni, galline, conigli,
e ogni tanto ci portava uno di questi cucinato, poi finì la
guerra il 1918 mio padre ritornò e tutto incomincio come
prima io avevo piu di 6 anni andavo a scuola faceva la prima
elementare, tutti quelli che erano andato dalle suore sapevano
fare l'alfabeto e tanti disegni. mio padre aveva prese tanti
clienti a fare le scarpe, con i soldi che guadagnava compro
altre terre e vigneti ci mettevano tanti operai a lavorare il 28
dicembre 1920 nacque mia sorella Assunta io avevo 7 anni era
contenta che aveva una sorella la cullava la puliva giocava con
lei in questo tempo mori il nonno cioe il padre di mia madre
mori da noi e noi sentimmo la sua mancanza perche ci volevo
tanto bene ci portava con lui quando andava in giro per il

paese a portare le carte delle tasse alla gente ma dopo un po'
di tempo mia madre cadde di nuovo ammalata ma questa volta
non era stanchezza era molto sciupata mio padre la portò dal
dottore del paese e a quei dei paesi vicini e nessuno di loro
indovinavano il male, poi andò a Napoli dal specialisti e dopo
tutto le analisi dissi che il sangue non circolava più i nervi si
erano ritirati aveva la apoplessia non cera più da fare con le
mani era paralizzata e la mandavano ogni anno ai bagni per
non farla peggiorare e così per me tutto campio io crescievo
ma era sempre ancora piccola per fare certi lavori dovevo
andare alla scuola, come ho detto che il mio paese era senza
comodita non vi era acqua potabile si dovevo andare alla
fontana per lavare la biancheria, non cerano panetteria per
comprare il pane ognuno se lo preparava in casa e poi si
portava al forno a cuocere, non cera luce eletrica si usavano
lumi a petrolio, mia madre mi insegnava a fare tante cose mi
dicevo quello che dovevo fare e io le facevo, il pane qualche
volta veniva una sorella più giovane di lei zia Antonia io
guardava come lo inbastava e cosi incominciai a farlo io ma le
mie mane erano piccole e ne facevo un po' alla volta. qualche
volta veniva mia cuggina che abbitava vicino a noi, una volta
mi ricordo che mi aiutò mio padre, non cerano lavandaie per
lavare la biancheria, si doveva lavare quasi tutti i giorni perché
cera mia sorella piccola, cera una donna che mia madre
conosceva questa andava tutti i giorni alla fontana a lavare la
biancheria ai signori e così mia madre la pagava io andavo
dopo scuola col secchietta della biancheria e questa donna mi
aiutava e mi guardava, mia madre non solo la pagava ma la
dava sempre qualche cosa per mangiare, io non mi lamentava
mai, per me non cerano mai giocattoli mai bambole la mia
bambola era mia sorella e giocava con lei mi ricordo che il mio
paese come ho detto allinizio non si conosciva nulla forse
erano tutti cosi i paesi del sud Italia, non avevano le usanze di

festegiare ne compleanni, ne onomastichi, e neanche cerano i
regali di Natale, era una festa grande si facevano le funzione in
chiesa si parlava della Befana, i genitori alla vigilia mettevano
le calze appeso al focolaio e ci mettevano qualche frutto
qualche ciocolata caramelle se eri stata buona, ma se eri stata
cattiva mettevano carbone e cenere, mi ricordo che ero
buona, che mia madre e tutte le sorelle e le cognate
preparavano i dolci le sfogliatelle le zeppole i strufoli e altri e
si mangiava tutti insieme e tutti facevano cosi, mi ricordo che
mia zia Colomba mi diede una cosa secca pareva una rosa e mi
diceva di metterla nellaqua alla vigilia se alla mattina di Natale
era aperta e fiorita si diceva che l'anno nuovo era buono
questa rosa la chiamavano, la rosa di Gerusalemme la mattina
tutte le mie cuggine venivano a casa per vedere se era fiorita
eravamo tutte contente, adesso anche l'altro nonno mori, ma
non nella mia casa, mori da zio Pietro, e non tanto sentimmo
la sua mancanza. il tempo passava avevo 10 anni mio fratello
piu grande di me aveva 12 anni aveva finito le scuole
elementare e se ne andò in collegio dai Padri domenicani ad
Arezzo, e così eravamo piu pochi in famiglia e cera anche per
me meno lavoro, facevo la 4 classe e nella scuola mi portavo
bene ci insegnavano pure a fare dei lavori, come a tirare i fili
vicino le stoffe per fare il punto a giorno, ci facevano fare gli
orli, e tante altre cose che mi piacevano tanto, che anche a
casa quando avevo tempo li facevo, mia madre mi insegnavo a
lavorare con luncinetto, avevo 11 anni e stavo per finire la
scuola, ma mio padre prego alla maestra di farmi ripetere la
classe cioè la 4 classe perche ero troppo piccola per lasciare la
scuola perche non cerano altre classe piu della 4 in questo
tempo venne il fascismo e tutti dovevano essere fascisti e cosi
anchio dovevo essere, alla mia età si chiamavano piccole
Italiane, avevamo la divisa facevamo le sfilate mi piaceva
tanto avevo tante compagne, ma dopo la scuola ero molto

occupata per aiutare mia madre a fare le facende di casa alla
sera facevo la lezione, e passavano i giorni, mi ricordo che
avevo una mania di rompere sempre qualche cosa non passava
un giorno, o rombevo un piatto o un bichiero rompevo tanti
tubi del lume a petrolio, mia madre mi voleva bene ma delle
volte mi sgridava e mi dicevo di star attenta, come ho detto
che alla scuola mi imparavo a fare tanti lavoretti ma dovevo
continuare a insegnarmi altre e a poco a poco mi imparai bene
di ricamare a mano ora la scuola era finita, non doveva più
studiare avevo tempo era piu cresciuta e mi toccavano i
lavori piu pesanti come ho detto che cerano le vigne si
mettevano tanti operai che zappavano si doveva portare da
mangiare a questi uomini che non erano mai meno di 10 11 al
giorno mia madre cucinavo per loro dovevano mangiare due
volte al giorno veniva sempre qualche moglia di questi operai
per portare la cesta col cucinato in campagna e mia madre che
come ho detto non poteva andare in campagna, me ne
preparavo una più piccolo per me, ma questi lavori pesanti
venivano di inverno faceva freddo non cerano ne cappotti si
usavano gli scialli non cerano guanti e per farmi stare calde le
mani mi metteva attorcigliato due tovaglioli piccolo della
cucina cosi le mani stavano calde per mantenere la cesta sul
capo, certo questo non succedeva sempre, così adesso che
aveva 13 14 anni mi doveva insegnare a cucire perche al mio
paese quase tutte le ragazze dovevano sapere qualche cosa di
cucito tranne le contadine mio madre si dispiaceva di me che
io non era libero come le mie compagne che andavano a
imparare di cucire e volevo a tutti i costi che anchio andassi
dalla sarta, aveva una cuggina figlia di un fratello di mio padre
che era sarta e cosi mia madre la pregò che mi insegnassi a
cucire certo io non potevo andare tutti i giorni come le altre,
ma io quando andavo ci mettevo tutto la volontà e cosi
facevo anchio i lavori che facevano le altre che andavano

tutti i giorni, le mie compagne quando mi vedevano arrivare
erano contento, anchio ero contenta che era con loro, e mi
domandavano se andassi il giorno dopo cosi potevamo fare
qualche cosa di speciale e dicevamo che ognuno portava
qualche cosa si preparavano dei pranzetti a me toccava
sempre a portare il vino mia cuggina ci faceva fare andavamo
in cucina perché sua madre era in campagna, suo padre era in
America, e questo lo facevamo sempre quando mia cuggina era
di buon umora, certe volte era di cattivo umore era arrabiata,
che aveva molto da fare e diceva che quel giorno cera molto
da fare si doveva lavorare aveva tanta clientela che ogni volta
che cera una festa si lavorava pure la notte una volta quel
giorno io non andai a cucire era dinverno cera la neve e le
ragazze che erano andate a cucire quando era mezzogiorno si
andava sempre per 5 minuti al castello a prendere un po' di
aria, e quel giorno videro un pollastro sperduto nella neve lo
presero lo partarono da una vecchia che stava vicino a mia
cugina e questa vecchia ci aiutava sempre a nascondere le cose
che portavamo per cucinare, ammazzo il pollo per noi, alla
sera una delle mie compagne venne a casa e disse a mia madre
che il giorno dopo dovevo andare a cucire che cera molto da
fare, e quando la mattina dopo che arrivai mi raccontarono il
fatto del pollo lo cucinammo con i maccheroni questo si
facevo spesse volte, ora era una ragazza e tutto era facile
tanto le facende di casa, a lavare la biancheria, a fare il pane,
un giorno pero il pane non tanto volle lievitare e quando lo
partai al forno non era cresciuto bene la fornaia mi sgridò mi
dissi che io non era buona a nulla, io mi misi a piangere cera
una vicina di casa che la rimproverò dissi che io faceva il pane
da piccola e non era il caso di farmi piangere perche anche alle
grande qualche volta non viene bene, si facevano sempre i
maccheroni a mano qualche volta si compravano, mia madre
mi aveva imparata a fare i cavatelli i fusilli i gnocchi e

cappelletti e la sfoglia per fare le tagliatelle, ma questa sfoglia
era un po' dificile, mi ricordo una volta che mia madre era ai
bagni mio padre era in campagna e io volevo fare la sfoglia e
non mi veniva bene mi misi a piangere non sapevo come fare
nello stesso tempo passò da casa mia cuggina e me la aiutò lei
a fare adesso anche mio fratello Angelo avevo finito la scuola
e si doveva imparare un mestiere si scelse falegnamo e anche
mia sorella andava a scuola ora anche loro facevano qualche
cosa mi ricordo in questo periodo venne la missione a
predicare per 15 giorni, il mio paese era molto religioso e tutti
si andava a sentire le prediche ogni sera per 15 giorni allora si
fondo il circolo Cattolica e tutte le ragazze cioe chi voleva
appartenere le mie amiche che ne avevo tanto, tutte si
scrissero a questa azione cattolica e anchio mi scrissi si
chiamavano la gioventu cattolica, e si dovevo andare tutte le
domenica dopo mezzogiorno a pregare, io non mancavo mai
mi alzava presto facevo tutto per essere libera, come ho detto
che quando andava a scuola era piccola Italiana adesso che ero
ragazza continuava appartenere ma ci chiamavano giovane
italiane non importa che avevo da fare ma appartenevo lo
stesso a queste organizazione, quando si doveva lavare la
biancheria specialmente durante lestate si andava al fiume ci
riunivamo tutte le compagne eravamo sempre 5 o 6
preparavamo tante cose per mangiare, si andava troppo
presto alla mattina, prima si lavava la biancheria si finiva
sempre verso 1 dopo mezzogiorno, i panni si stendevano al
sole sullerba per asciugare, e noi giocavamo si mangiava ci
facevamo i bagni nel fiume si cantava era come una
scampagnata eravamo tutte felice ci riunivamo ogni 15 giorni
durante l'inverno si andava alla fontana ma solo per lavare e
sempre era cosi non avevamo altre divertimenti non cera
niente ne cinema non si usciva mai, non si dava retta a nessun
ragazzo, se qualcuna faceva la civetta era una cattiva ragazza,

mai si usciva di sera non cerano radio non televisione, come
ho detto che avevamo i vigneti, facevamo 70-80 quintali di
vino all'anno, e durante la vendemmia cera molto da lavorare,
le donne che vendemmiavano, gli uomini che con i muli che
portavano luva a Cairano, avevamo una grande candina, si
portava con i muli perché non cerano altri mezzi per portala,
alla sera cerano altri uomini che la dovevano pigiare, si
pigiava con i piedi nelle grande tine, gli uomini si lavavano i
piedi, si mettevano i calzoni corti per pigiare, e tutto questo
lavora durava 15 20 giorni, ma per preparare il vino ci voleva
piu di un mese, per me era pure molto lavoro, dovevo andare
in campagna con le donne dovevo portare il mangiare cera
tanta allegria con loro cantavano le canzoni della vendemmia
quando alla sera si ritornava a Cairano tutte le contadine si
riunivano durante la via quella che andavano a seminare il
grano, quelle che andavano a vendemmiare, e cantavano,
ridevano, e cosi era pure durante il raccolto del grano fave
grandurco e altre cose, come ho detto che noi avevamo i
coloni, ma al raccolto si doveva aiutare un pò, io ogni giorno
dopo mezzogiorno andavo per prendere la metà del raccolto
che toccava a noi, ma poi mio padre non volle fare piu il
calzolaio perche le tasse che dovevo pagare per il mestiero
non gli rendevano, e cosi si diede piu alla campagna cioè solo
ai vigneti, il vino che facevamo lo vendeva allingrosso cioe
venivano i compratori da lontano, e un po' lo vendevo anche
al minuto nel nostro paese, la nostra casa era al centro del
paese proprio in piazza era composta di una grande stanza al
primo piano a fianco dove avevo lavorato mio padre poi non
lavorava piu avevo fatto una piccola cucina, al secondo piano
cerano altre 4 stanze 3 da letto e uno era come un salotto
dove si riunivano spesso gli amici di mio padre venivano quei
4 signori e giocavano a carte a tre sette la scopa che chi
perdeva pagava il vino che si giocavano, lo facevano per

passare il tempo, spesso facevano le conversazione mia madre
cucinava io aiutavo cerano dei amici che erano cacciatori e
spesse portavano gli uccelli lepre e altre animale che
prendevano portavano pescie che pescavano uova e tante
altre cose mi ricordo che cera una famiglia che abitavano in
campagna, mia madre aveva fatto due volte la commare di
battezzo a due dei loro figli, e ogni domenica mattina
venivano al paese per andare alla messa e per comprare
qualche cosa, e dovevano passare davanti alla nostra casa e
ogni volta chiamavano a mia madre per darle quando dei
conigli galletti uova formaggi non passavano mai che non
portavano qualche cosa, come ho detto che vendevamo il
vino al minuto la nostra cantina era pure vicino alla nostra
casa, e quando venivano quelle che compravano al minuto
spesso toccava a me di andare in cantina per darlo. vi era una
donna povera vicina e quando vedevo che andavo io veniva
con un grande bicchiero e mi chiedevo un po' di vino, io ce lo
dava sempre, ce nera tanto, come vedete il tempo passava io
crescieva adesso di cucire e ricamare a mano mi avevo
imparato discretamente, mia madre diceva che mi doveva
imparare a lavorare coi ferri per fare le maglie e le calze, ma
le maglie me le imparai ma le calze non volle impararre, dissi
che le facevano solo le vecchie, volevo imparare a ricamare a
macchina. la macchina mio padre me laveva comprata che io
non sapeva ancora cucire, aveva avuto una occasione e laveva
pagata a metà prezzo, aveva una compagna di scuola vicino
alla mia casa che a dire la verità era un po' orgogliosa perche
era unica figlia stava sempre sola non si univa mai a noi, si
facevo più alta di noi. aveva il nonno in America che
mandava tanti soldi, il padre aveva un fratello a S. Maria
Capua vicino Napoli la moglie sapeva ricamare a macchina e
la mandarono da loro per farla imparare a ricamare dopo 3
mesi ritornò a Cairano era cosi contenta che sola essa sapeva

ricamare a macchina al paese, allora io la domandai se mi
voleva imparare mia madre la voleva pagare ma dissi di no che
non avrebbe insegnato a nessuno, io volevo a tutti i costi
insegnarmi cera una donna che sapeva un po' ma non
lavorava perché era sempre ammalata mia madre la domandò
se volessi insegnarmi prima disse di no perche non si sentiva
ma poi mi prese andai una settimana ogni giorno mi insegnava
a fare un punto diverso ma dopo che era finito quello che
sapeva mi dissi che adesso mi doveva perfezionare da sola, e
cosi quando avevo tempo stava sempre vicino alla macchina e
in poco tempo mi imparai bene, quando lo seppe questa mia
compagna si arrabiò e volevo sapere chi mi aveva insegnato io
non ce lo dissi perche quella signora mi aveva detto di non
dirle a nessuno. come ho detto prima che non cera luce
eletrica, adesso era venuto dall'America un signore che aveva
portati tanti soldi e incomingio a fare procetti per portare la
luce al paese dato che questo aveva anche il mulino per fare la
farina e funzionava a olio era molto pericoloso una volta mori
una donna e con leletricità era piu meglio e cosi in poco
tempo arrivò la luce, io mi ricordo che dopo fatto tutto
impiando nel paese quel giorno si doveva dare la
illuminazione, a mia casa la sera tutti i amici di mio padre non
ho detto che mio padre era pure consigliere al municipio
avevano una conversazione mia madre aveva cucinato tante
cose io laveva aiutata, e cera pure il sindaco allora prego al
contrattore che mettesse un filo provvisorio che portasse la
luce dentro per potersi divertire meglio cosi la prima casa del
paese che ebbi la luce fu la nostra io era cosi contenta e restò
cosi fino che poi venne leletricista a mettere limpiando per
tutta la casa avevo 16-17 anni ormai ero una giovane e mia
madre mi diceva che doveva incominciare a fare il corredo che
cosi si usava, tutte le ragazze dovevano farsi il corredo, mia
madre dato che era malata aveva fretta che mi facessi il

corredo mi comprava la stoffa diceva che adesso che di cucire
mi avevo imparata e anche di ricamare poteva lavorare,
cerano tanti ragazzi che mi facevano la corte ma io non dava
retta a nessuno non era ancora tempo, anche i miei genitori
dicevano che era presto, cera un ragazzo che i suoi genitori
volevano per me e venivano sempre a casa dato che erano
pure amici di mio padre e mia madre e ne parlavano con loro
ma i miei dissero che dovevano aspettare almeno un anno io
non sapeva nullo il ragazzo veniva spesso con loro ed e
proprio questo che mi sono sposato io non volevo nessuno
attorno a me mi piaceva come stava tanto nessuno delle
compagne avevano il ragazzo, ma mia madre era molto amica
con la madre non voleva dire di nuovo che non era tempo,
perche gia avevano detto un altra volta, ma doveva venire
non piu di due volte alla settimana a casa, come ho detto
prima che apparteneva alle giovane fasciste a quelle cattoliche
e tutte le mie compagne o che erano invidiose e per che cosa
mi dicevano che avevo il ragazzo io arrossiva e mi arrabiava
con mia madre, il 1930 nel mese di agosto di notte non
ricordo la dato mi ricordo che era verso l'una io ero sveglia e
aveva la luce acceso perche volevo vedere lora perche la
mattina mi doveva alzare presto perche io e le mie compagne
dovevamo andare al fiume ha lavare la biancheria e vidi il
lampadario in mezzo alla stanza che si muoveva anche i quadri
che erano apeso al muro e subito mi misi a gridare che era il
terremoto non so come mi venne di dire che tremavo perche
non avevo mai visto, tutto la gente usci fuori dalle case ma
non fece niente, per diverse sera andavamo fuori dal paese per
paura, mia sorella assunta aveva 10 anni si metteva paura e
ogni sera di prendeva il cuscino sotto il braccio piangeva che
voleva andare via ma dopo 8 giorni non usciva piu di casa,
mio padre dato che non lavorava piu da calzolaio, cosi lui e un
suo amico volevano fare qualche cosa e decisero di comprare

tutte le concime nitrato per concimare i terreni, solfato di rame zolfo per le vigne, perche tutti la dovevamo comprare in altri paesi vicini, e cosi un altro lavoro per me, mio padre fece bandire nel paese che chi voleva comprare tutte le concime che li servivano si doveva venire a dire, io dovevo scrivere nel quaderno il loro nome e la quantità e dopo che tutto avevano venuto di dire quando ne volevano, mio padre mandava al consorzio a montecatini la quandità che volevo, e cosi quando arrivavano i carri merci alla stazione si doveva andare a prendere, e di nuovo si bandiva che tutti quelle che avevano ordinati dovevano andare a ritirarla io dovevo andare con mio padre perche dovevo chiamare tutti i loro nomi e non erano poche piu di 1000 quintali, tutto questo lavoro toccava a me, perche come ho detto mio fratello piu grande di me era al collegio dai monaci, l'altro piu piccolo di me era in unaltro paese a perfezionarsi il mestiere da falegname perche aveva andato da un falegname del nostro paese, ma volevo imparare di piu, mia sorella era piccola e cosi io dovevo fare tutto, le facende di casa, andare in campagna a portare da mangiare gli operai quando venivano a lavorare nelle vigne, a prendere la metà del raccolto dai coloni quando avevo tempo dovevo lavorare nel prepararmi il correto, non ho piu parlato della malattia di mia madre ma piu passavo il tempo e piu peggiorava, piu si dimagriva i dottori non potevano fare niente, con questo ritmo passava il tempo, non ricordo l'anno ma venne un morbo ai vigneti in poco tempo tutte le vigne caddero malato gli esperti non sapevano che era ma poi se seppe che era una malattia chiamata la filosafo non cera niente che si poteva fare, mi ricordo che quando mettevamo gli operai per zappare mio padre accendeva un fuoco e faceva passare le zappe dei operai per disinfettare ma non si ricavava niente, e in poco tempo il male distrusse tutte le vigne non solo del nostro paese ma di tutta l'Italia e forse tutto Europa,

noi avevamo un pezzetto di vigneto era sola anzi era
attaccato con i miei zii che avevano pure loro la vigna, non si
sa se non cerano altre vigne vicino o come che mantenne un
po' piu a lungo, e cosi, mio padre volle fare un po' di vigna
nuova mise gli operai a preparare il terreno ma per mettere le
vite si dovevano comprare le vite americane, non so se le
chiamavano cosi o pure venivano veramente dallamerica, ma
ci volevo molto lavoro e dovevano passare almeno 3 anni se
tutto andava bene per avere la vigna e per questo non
avevamo piu tante vigne, questo anche a me mi dispiaceva e
mi sentiva anche in colpa perche quando avevamo tutte quelle
vigne cera tanto lavoro specialmente quando si vendemmiava
io mi arrabiavo e dicevo spesso che se seccavano era meglio,
non cera tanto lavoro, sai perche, perche si vendemiava alla
fine di ottobre e alla mattina si doveva andare presto in
campagna nelle vallate vicino al fiume Ofanto cera sempre la
nebbia e faceva freddo le mani quasi si ghiacciavano poi usciva
il sole e incominciava a far caldo venivano le api perche cera
tanta uva ammuchiata tanto mosto che scorreva le api mi
pizzicavano mi facevano gonfiare le mani, non solo a me ma
anche alle donne che raccoglevano luva, e percio adesso che i
vigneti si erano seccati mi sentiva male e diceva forse era
stata io che li avevo fatto seccare, ma certo non era vero
perche erano tutte ammalate, mamma sempre andava più
male, pensava sempre a mio fratello lontano desideravo di
vederlo, allora facemmo un telegramma che mia madre stava
male, e così venne per 4 giorni, ma quando arrivò si mise a
piangere nel vedere la mamma come si era sciupata che non la
conoscieva piu, adesso si avvicinava il tempo che mio fratello
doveva prendere la messa, mia madre pregava che il signore la
davo la contentezza che prima che morisse vedesse suo figlio
sacerdote, cosi lanno dopo prese la messa i miei genitori erano
cosi contento e prepararono una festa con un grande

banghetto invitarono tutti i signori del paese gli amici e
parenti vennero dei cuochi per preparare i piatti di diversi
specie dolci liquori vini imbottigliati che preparava mio padre
due o 3 anni prima questa festa venne il estate proprio del
mese di giugno era di domenica tutto il paese ando in chiesa
era mio fratello e un altro che dicevano la prima messa mia
madre non poteva camminare, ma piano piano la portarono
mio padre tutti gli invitati io restai a casa, mia madre come
piangeva, e ringraziava al signore che laveva dato quel dono,
mio fratello resta a Cairano un mese, ogni mattina andava a
dire la messa e anche mia madre piano piano andava ma in
questo tempo che restò con noi parlavano di mia sorella
Assunta, mia madre che si sentiva prossima a morire, diceva
che mio fratello ormai era sacerdote, io fra qualche anno mi
sposava angelo era pure grande, ma Assunta era piu piccola
aveva 12 anni, e cosi mio fratello volevo che andassi dalle
suore ma mia sorella non volevo andare dicevo che non si
voleva vestire da suora non lo piaceva, e mio fratello la disse
che dove la voleva che andassi non era un convento ma un
Istituto che studiavano per diventare insegnante e non si
vestivano da suora ma da signorina e cosi disse che ci andava e
così a ottobre l'anno dopo ci preparammo il corredo
personale e vestiti e parti, mia madre era quasi passato piu di
un anno e in questo tempo era piu pegiorato, era diventata
pelle e ossa e dato che il sangue non circolava piu le dite erano
tutte curve che i nervi si erano ritirati si aggiunse un altro
male gli uscivano tutti punti neri e gli davano tanto dolore,
non poteva riposare tutte le notti stava sveglio e si lamentava
dal dolore, io che dormivo alla stanza accanto alla sua anchio
stavo sveglio e pregavo al signore che la facesse riposare e con
tutte queste sofferenze non impregava male contro il destino,
solo ogni tanto diceva signore forse ti o messo io sulla croce,
non voleva che nessuno si dispiaceva per lei, se qualcuna la

veniva a trovare perche non poteva piu uscire gli diceva
poveretta come e ridotto lei si mortificava voleva che la
dicessero cose allegra stava sempre con la corona a dire rosarii
ma nessuno sentiva, io la dovevo aiutare a vestire e volevo
che assolutamente mi sposassi prima che morisse avevo tanta
fretta che mi finisse il correto e cosi incominciarono i
preparativo per il mio matrimonio, ma non mi vide sposare,
era il 1934 il 3 marzo un sabato io come ha detto che ero
giovane cattoliche e in quel periodo si facevano i 15 sabati alla
madonna di Pompei e io li facevo pure come le mie
compagne, alle nove quando ritornai dalla chiesa mia madre
mi disse che si avrebbe pettinata i capelli e io ci dovevo fare le
trecce perche lei non le poteva fare, ce li facevo sempre io,
quando mi dissi cosi parlava bene, ma dopo pochi minuti non
poteva piu parlare le aveva preso la paralisi subito
chiamammo il dottore ma non cera piu da fare io era sola
Angelo mio fratello era in bottega a lavorare lo chiamai mio
padre era andato in campagna a legare le viti subito lo
mandammo a chiamare ma quando arrivò era gia morta, aveva
53 anni le ultime parole che dissi che volevo Gesu chisto, cioe
la comunione, ma non fece in tempo subito si seppe per il
paese e anche per la campagna perche chi moriva prima di
mezzogiorno suonavano le campane a lutto, e dato che il
postino a quell'ora andava alla stazione a prendere la posta lo
domandavano disse che era morta Filomena Grassi lo seppero
quelli che lavoravano le nostre terre, e subito ritornarono a
Cairano vennero a casa, alla sera tutti accorsero a casa per far
visita i funerali durarono 3 giorni mio fratello Michelangelo
arrivò il giorno dopo che mia madre era morta e lui gli fece i
funerali. mia madre era molto conosciuta da tutto il paese
vennero tutti ai funerali, cosi mia madre non cera piu, la casa
era vuota, pure essenta molta malata ma volevamo che stava
ancora con noi, mio fratello Angelo piangeva sempre se ne

andava nella sua stanza e piangeva io dicevo che non doveva
piangere, ma lui diceva che quando io mi sposava lui restava
solo e pensava che mio padre si risposava aveva 56 anni era
ancora giovane, ma non lo fece rispetto mia madre si vesti di
nero per tanto tempo e se qualcuno lo diceva che si togliesse
quella camicia nera lui rispondeva se avrebbe morto lui mia
madre avrebbe portato lo stesso lutto per tutto la vita, per piu
di 6 mese non si riuniva piu con i amici per giocare come
faceva prima, pensò a finire il mio corredo, penso per tutto
quello che occorreva per il mio matrimonio, cera questa mia
cuggina che lo aiuto a tutto, per me dopo la morte di mia
madre tante cose finirono come Gioventu Cattolica fascisti io
ero mortificato, e ogni giorno che passavo dicevo mia madre
non cera piu, e inutile continuare, adesso si avvicinava il
tempo che mi dovevo sposare ma io non ero contenta, non
voleva lasciare la mia casa mio fratello e mio padre erano due
uomini soli, mio fratello Michelangelo era ritornato in
convento, mia sorella non era venuto alla morte di mia madre
perche non era permesso, e per non darle dispiacere non
avevamo fatto sapere nulla, lo seppe dopo, cosi dopo 10 mesi
arrivò il tempo perche mi dovevo sposare ma io ero sempre
mortificata perché era perduto la mia madre. cera una zia
tanto a noi che alla famiglia del mio fidanzato che si
occuparono di tutto quello che mi occorreva, io non volle
neanche andare a comprarmi neanche il vestito bianco, dissi
come lo volevo gli detti le misure e me lo comprarono loro,
perche al mio paese si usava che il vestito della sposa lo
doveva comprare la madre del fidanzato, si comprava pure
l'oro era tutto come un regalo, mi conbrarono il vestito e
tutto lacconciatura mi conbrarono una bella collana un
orologio a bracciale una spilla tutto oro di 18 carati e tutto era
bello, e mi piaceva. io come ho detto che dopo la morte di
mia madre avevo smesso di appartenere alle gioventu

cattolica, ma le volevo salutare perche dopo non era piu
giovane ma donna cattolica, allora si riunirono in chiesa
lultima domenica e io gli portai i confetti e loro tutte insieme
avevano comprato un bel regalo un servizio di pendole per la
cucina. e cosi il 3 gennaio 1935 alle dieci di mattina mi sposai
mi sposo mio fratello venne solo per sposarmi ma dopo pochi
giorni riparti mia sorella non venne perche non la facevano
venire non andammo in viaggio di nozze perché tanto non
andavano, ma dopo un po' di tempo andammo per qualche
giorno a Napoli Pompei cosi la mia vita era campiata, prima
alla mia casa si puo dire che ero io che faceva tutto a mio
piacere, che volevo cucinare come fare le facente, pensavo
alla mia casa, era restato mio padre e Angelo mio fratello, io
andavo a fare qualche cosa, ma loro piano piano si adattavano
si cucinavano io gli lavavo la biancheria e per me era un
dispiacere, la mia vita nuova era un po' buona e in po' brutto,
dovevo servire ai miei suoceri perche stavamo con loro
perche cosi si usava che lultimo figlio doveva restare con i
genitori ma a me non piaceva era tutto diverso io dovevo fare
tutto, mia suocera solo che si preoccupava per la cucina era
tutto diferente come si mangiava a casa mia mi dovevo
abituare ma a me non tanto mi piaceva e neanche a mio
marito piaceva, se lavorava del suo mestiere doveva
consegnare i soldi a suo padre e quando non cera lavoro
andava in campagna, se io facevo qualche lavoro di cucito a
qualcuno lo dovevo dare a mia suocera, noi non avevamo mai
un soldo non avevamo piu ne io tutte quelle compagne, e
neanche mio marito, un giorno venne una discussione un
litigio, mio suocero era arrabiato e disse che se non ci piaceva
come si stava ce ne andavamo, mio marito subito usci e trovò
un piccolo appartamento vuoto e quel giorno stesso ce ne
dovevamo andarci, io mi misi a piangere non mi piaceva di
stare, ma neanche volevo andarmene, subito vennero due

cugine di mio marito e una mia cugina e portarono via le
nostre cose tanto non erano molto avevamo solo la stanza da
letto e qualche altre cosette, i amici di mio marito subbito alla
sera ci vennero a trovare erano cosi contenti ci aiutarono a
mettere a posto tutto ci portarono qualche cosa da mangiare e
passo, mio marito era contento perche poteva fare tutto
come voleva, non piu come un figlio, adesso era sposato e
aveva il diritto di fare qualche cosa a suo piacere, avere gli
amici, anchio mi sentivo meglio certo non avevamo nulla ma
eravamo contento il giorno dopo dovevamo preparare qualche
cosa da mangiare avevamo solo due casseruole e mi ricordo
che il primo giorno cucinammo le tagliatelle ma non avevamo
con che mangiarle cera una cuggina di mio marito vicino a
casa e andò da lei e si fece dare due forchette per mangiarle il
giorno apresso era il 24 giugno cera una fiera ad Andretta, un
paese vicino al nostro avevamo un po' di soldi, e andammo e
ci comprammo tutti gli utensili che ci servivano, e cosi
incomiciò la nostra vita a due, i genitori di mio marito ci
portarono del grano mio padre ci porto altre cose era
dispiaciuto che eravamo andato via, ma noi eravamo contenti,
non stavamo mai soli tutti le mie amiche gli amici di mio
marito stavano sempre da noi, specialmente alla sera si
giocava a carte portavano qualche cosa da mangiare e qualche
cosa da bere, cera un mio cuggino Michelangelo era prima di
me e veniva tutte le sere come pure un amico di mio marito
tutte le sere anche lui, qualche volta si vergognavano che
venivano tutte le sere, e ci dicevano di trovarci qualche
fidanzata, cosi non venivano sempre da noi, si facevano
spesso dei pranzi perche cerano altri amici e amiche e chi
portava una cosa e chi unaltra si cucinava si mangiava si
rideva facevano tanti scherzi quello che mi aiutava a cucinare
era un amico di mio marito si chiamava Gerardo e
specialmente quando facevamo i ravioli mi diceva che li

dovevamo fare di tante grandezze per far ridere a tutti, delle
volte qualche sera eravamo soli, e subito arrivavano loro con
qualche cosa da mangiare e si faceva tanto caciarra, eravamo
felici, pur non avendo niente certo adesso avevamo un po' di
terra che ci aveva dato il padre a mio marito perche cosi si
usava, il padre del fidanzato se ne aveva, doveva dare un po' di
terra, e il padre della fidanzata doveva dare la dote cioe
denaro, e il corredo, certo tutto e due come potevano con le
loro possibilità finanziarie, e cosi i figli comingiavano la loro
famiglia, e cosi dovevamo pure andare in campagna quando
cerano i lavori, delle volte anche i nostri amici ci venivano ad
aiutare, andavamo sempre nei santuari con questi amici e
amiche, quando venivano le feste, alla madonna delle Puglie a
S. Michele al monte gargano alla fiera di S. Giovanni alla
madonna dell'Incoronata, ma non solo per visitare i santi, che
nel nostro paese cera tanta devozione ma poi dopo fatto in
nostro dovere in chiese, ci divertivamo tutti avevamo portato
i cestini con qualche cosa da mangiare era come una
scampagnata, si stava bene cosi tutti insieme, io avevo ripreso
di nuovo a fare come le altre la devozione alla madonna di
Pompei faceva di nuovo i 15 sabati come le mie compagne
quando avevo un po' di tempo andavo alle riunioni con loro
mi ricordo, che proprio vicino alla nostra casa cerano due
fratelli Nicola, e Pasquale, per non farsi vedere dai loro
genitori che venivano tutte le sere a casa, qualche sera
dicevano che volevano andare a dormire e non si andavano
accomodavano il letto con le coperte e i cuscini come se cera
qualcuno che dormiva si toglievano le scarpe e venivano a
casa per giocare con gli altri, delle volte questi due amici
avevano da un loro parente del vermut a poco prezzo e lo
portavano e lo pagavano un po' ciascuno, cera un amico lui
era il figlio di un banchiero e lui portava sempre tanta roba
questa volta era il giorno dopo pasqua e in Italia fanno tutti

festa, questo giorno si chiama pasquetta, mi ricordo che portò
un capretto e lo doveva ammazzare lui stesso ma per
amazzarlo ne compinò tanto si poteva dire che si divertiva
per ammazzarlo questo era sempre che scherzava, e morto in
venezuela tanto giovane che quando lo sapemmo ci dispiacque
tanto si chiamava Don Alessio, era un maestro di musica, e
inutile continuare altre cose, stavamo bene, quando si dovevo
andare a lavorare in campagna si andava, e quando si dovevo
lavorare al paese, mio marito da falegname e io pure cuciva
qualche cosa con gli altri, tutto era normale andavamo a
visitare ai genitori, ma tutto questo non durò molto a lungo,
non so di preciso ma so che mio suocero certo sapeva che
eravamo contento che cerano tutti questi amici, perche come
o detto che il paese era piccolo si sapeva tutto si arrabio e
disse che quel tutto quello, non avevamo voluto stare con loro
e comincio il disturbo che veniva qualche lite e non eravamo
piu contento come prima gli amici e amiche venivano lo
stesso ma non facevamo come prima, era la vigilia di Natale e
dovevamo andare da i miei suoceri a mangiare ma io era
dispiaciuto che mio padre era solo, ma andai lo stesso ma per
me non era la vigilia come dovevo essere mangiammo e dopo
un po' di tempo dissi che volevo andare a casa perché avevo il
male di testa, ma non era vero, mio marito non trovo nulla di
contrario che ci dovevamo ritirare, poco dopo che eravamo a
casa subito vennero certo amici e ci trattennero un po' piu
allegri cosi passò puro il giorno di Natale il primo dell'anno, io
non ho detto che ero incinta e nel mese di marzo cioe i primi
di marzo nacque una bambina mori mentre nascieva, tutto
questo venne che non cerano ne Dottore e ne levatrice,
durante il parto, ma cera una donna che ne sapeva un po' e
quando venne il Dottore era morta, io non la vidi ma dicevano
che era una bella bambina la misero il nome di mia madre
Filomena, certo io ero dispiaciuta ma piano piano passava ma

quando vedevo due mie compagne che erano sposato con me,
anche loro avevano avuto due bambine mi sembrava brutto, e
così eravamo soli noi due, il tempo scorrevo un po' buono un
po' brutto, col lavoro della campagna e cioe del raccolto si
mangiava, e con quello che lavoravamo nel nostro mestiero ci
compravamo di quel che ci bisognava per la casa, qualche
fornitura e tutto il resto così incominciavamo a sistemarci piu
bene, avevamo sempre gli stessi amici, andavamo sempre a
qualche santuario come era lusanza, qualche volta io andavo in
campagna dai genitori di mio marito per aiutarli a quello che
potevo fare, ma mio suocero con me era sempre indiferente,
qualche volta andavo a casa di mio padre a fargli qualche cosa,
tanto adesso era restato solo perche mio fratello Angelo se ne
era andato in avviazione aveva fatto una domanda e cera
venuto accettato, Michelangelo era dai monaci, mia sorella
era in istituto, e quando venivano io andavo a casa per
cucinare, mio fratello Michelangelo gli piacevano le tagliatelle
all'uovo e tante altre cose che si usavano a casa, perche dai
Frati non li mangiava mai, adesso era di nuovo incinta e nel
mese di aprile il 21 1937 nacque Raffaele, questa volta tutto
andò bene, allora cera la levatrice diplomata, e non appena mi
sentii male mio marito andò a chiamarla questa era una
appena laureata era una ragazza era di Venezia si chiamava
Ines, ma era troppo attaccata ai giovani, e non si trovava mai
quando la volevano, il giorno prima una donna doveva avere il
bambino ma lei non si poteva trovare perche era in giro con
qualcuno e il bambino mori, cosi mio marito gli dissi che se
non veniva subbito e se succedeva qualche cosa lei passava dei
guai e subito venne, stette sempre a casa, io ridevo e gli dicevo
che era solo qualche dolore, io gli stavo lavorando due centrini
a ricamo cosi io lavoravo e lei mi guardava il bambino naque
alle 6 di sera tutto andò bene il bambino era in buona salute.
dopo 8 giorni lo battezzammo il suo nome come ho detto

Raffaele, perche nel mio paese il primo bambino che viene se
e maschio si chiamo come il padre del padre del bambino e
mio suocero era contento che si era rinnovato il suo nome,
perche non ne avevano avuto altri due figli, e anche con me
era piu gentile, dopo un po' il bambino cadde ammalato e tutte
le cure non gli giovavano, non cerano come oggi tante cose
per nutrirlo tutti davano il latte materno e il mio latte era
molto pesante io non potevo mangiare niente, ma solo roba
leggera, ma dopo un po' passo bene e si fece subbito forte che
quando aveva 3 mesi sembrava che ne avesse 6, io gli avevo
preparato un bel correto tutto ricamato lo vestiva sempre
bene cerano 3 nipote che se lo venivano a prendere al giorno
per portarlo in giro e tutti lo guardavano, gli aveva fatto una
fascia all'uncinetto perche si fasciavano i bambini e una volta
una donna era di un paese vicino mi aveva detto che chi ha del
pepe lo mette pure nei cavoli, io non capivo che volevano
significare quelle parole, e mi dissi che noi avevamo molti
soldi che avevo fatto la fascia alluncinetto che non ne avevo
mai visto. io gli rispose che non avevamo soldi ma era stato il
mio tempo e un po di cotone per farlo. il bambino crescieva
noi lavoravamo e si tirava avanti gli amici e amiche chi si
sposava chi non ancora, ma eravamo sempre vicini uno con
laltro, quelle che come noi si erano sposati avevano anche
loro un po' di terra e facevamo i lavori insieme quando
venivano loro a lavorare con noi, e quando andavamo noi con
loro, e cosi il lavoro era un passa tempo specialmente quando
era tempo di raccolta quando si mieteva il grano cera tanta
allegria, dopo 2 anni cioe nel 1939 il 27 aprile ebbi un altro
bambino, anche questa volta tutto andò bene, ma non cera piu
quella levatrice il municipio la mandò via perche non faveva il
suo dovere andava sempre in giro come o detto prima, questa
era piu buona aveva più di 30 anni era di Napoli si chiamava
Bianca, ora avevo due bambini aveva piu da fare, ogni due

giorni dovevo lavare tutti i loro pannolini, si doveva andare
alla fontana perché come o detto prima che non cera aqua nel
paese, e mentre io andavo alla fontana li guardava mio marito,
ma 4 mesi dopo mio marito fu chiamato sotto le armi per 70
giorni per far istruzione, ma nel 1940 scoppiò la seconda
guerra montiale e cosi mio marito non torno, furono tutti
richiamati mio marito gia si trovava in libia, rimasero solo
donni e vecchi. anche i miei fratelli erano richiamati in guerra
Michelangelo faceva il cappellano dato che era sacerdote e
Angelo nellaviazione non so che faceva. adesso tutti i nostri
amiche e amici si erano tutti sposati e cosi rimanemmo tutte
sole, ma continuammo a essere sempre insieme, andavamo a
lavorare la campagna un giorno per parte, tante cose non
sapevamo fare ma piano piano ci imparammo, e neanche
capivamo che succedeva della guerra, non cerano radio, non
cerano giornali, si sapeva qualche cosa da quei pochi signori
che si compravano il giornale da lontani, noi che non
capivamo nulla eravamo tutti all'oscuro le lettere che
avevamo non dicevano molto, tutto cambio io veramente
come ho detto della guerra non so che succedeva, ma il
governo in poco tempo si ritirò tutte gli udenzili di rama per
far armi, tutto l'oro che avevamo perfino la fede nuziale, ti
dava un anello di bronzo, si ritirava tutto il grano ti dava 16
chili di grano a persona, ci dava un libretto si chiamava la
tessera, che cera scritto tutto quello che doveva avere, come
zucchero, olio, sale, e altre, non potevi comprare quello che
volevi ne stoffe ne scarpe, e tante altre cose che ti
occorrevano, col grano quelli che erano tutti persone grande
specialmente quelle contadine che lavoravano forte era poco,
perché con 16 kg di grano quando era fatta la farina non
poteva abbastare un mese intere, perche quello era tutto, non
cerano maccherone, se qualcuno avevo dei cereali, non era
tanto brutto, come quelli che avevano i bambini era sufficiente

ma non bastava lo zucchero e cosi si faceva cambio, tu che
avevi i bambini e il grano era molto davi a loro, e loro ti
davano lo zucchero, quando avevamo finito i vestiti che
avevamo non cera stoffa per comprarla, i negozi, che
lavevano se lavevano tutti conservata, e cosi chi aveva dei
lenzuoli sufficienti si prendeva il colore che lo piaceva si
tingevano e si facevano i vestiti, non cera sapone per lavare la
biancheria e nemeno per lavare noi, ci avevamo imbarato noi
a farlo ma si dovevo comprare una polvere non mi ricordo
come si chiama si prendevo del grasso e si metteva a bollire e
quando era raffreddata diventavo a sapone ma quando lo
avevamo il grasso lo facevamo. ci mancava tutto perfino i
fiamiferi per accendere il fuoco, mi ricordo che sotto alla mia
casa cera una famiglia contadina che tenevano sempre il fuoco
acceso notte e giorno, non so come facevano, ogni sera
mettevano un pezzo di legno duro sotto la cenere e cosi la
mattina trovavano sempre il fuoco acceso, erano tanta buona
gente che ogni mattina mi chiamavano di andare a prendere il
fuoco, cera il contrabando se volevo qualche cosa da tutti i
negozi come ho detto che si erano tutti conservate li doveva
pagare 3 volte il costo che era, e cosi tutto il resto e inutile
continuare, si diceva che la guerra chi moriva e chi si
arricchiva, andavano a fermare carri di treni li saccheggiavano
si prendevano tutti che cera non si poteva avere sale si
mangiava senza sale e tutto questo fino alla fine, quando
cerano i bombardamenti tutti stavano in casa, anche i
contadini andavano presto in campagna lavoravano fino alle
dieci e si ritiravano, perche il cielo era tutto pieno di areoplani
e gettavano bombe, mi ricordo che un giorno non potevo
trovare a Peppino il bambino piu piccolo e lo trovai sulla
strada che guardava come sparavano, gli piaceva tanto a
guardare come si vedevano lontano quando bombardavano
carri armati incendiavano le foreste, una notte io sentii un via

vai nella strada cavalli che passavano, io non sapevo che era
ma neanche volevo vedere, e alla mattina mi dissero che alla
stazione avevano saccheggiato un treno si avevano preso
tutto e una cuggina di mio marito e due vicine di casa dissero
che anche loro volevano andare a vedere se potevano
prendere anche loro qualche cosa andai pure io con loro ma
non ci trovammo niente, mentre che tornavamo
comingiarono di nuovo a bombardare e per poco non mi colpì
una scheggia di mitragliatrice. quando poi furono presi
prigionieri non si sapeva piu nulla, noi andavamo dalle croce
rosse per sapere qualche cosa ma non sapevamo mai nulla.

non sapevamo se erano morti o vivi, andavamo fine dalle
donne che dicevano che indovinavano dove erano ma ci
rubavano solo soldi, io prendevo poco piu di 200 lire al mese,
avevo due bambini mio marito era sergente maggiore, che
potevo fare con soldi cosi poco, dovevo comprare qualche
cosa per i bambini, per me non ci pensavo, adesso loro
crescievano ci volevo di piu, era sola dovevo andare in
campagna a lavorare qualche volta li lasciava dai nonni ma
non ci volevano stare il piu grande diceva che il nonno lo
sgridava sempre, me li portava con me quando dovevo stare
tutto il giorno, mi ricordo che un giorno nel mese di maggio li
avevo portato con me e venne un brutto temporale, facevano
lampi tuono la grandine, io avevo paura e anche loro
piangevano, il terreno era un po lontano dalla via che portava
al paese, tutta aqua, e per non lasciare uno di loro, perche
l'altro lo volevo portare alla strada me ne mise una sulle spalle
e l'altro in braccio e li portai alla strada quando arrivammo
eravamo tutti abagnati io non ce la faceva piu cosi era una
vitaccia, quando dovevo mettere dei operai ma erano tutti
vecchi, veniva sempre mio padre per vigilarli che lavorassero,
mi ricordo che quando ero in estate adesso erano piu grandi, e
io dovevo raccogliere tante cose come faggioli ceci altre cose

come le spighe per terra dopo che si aveva mietuto il grano si
doveva andare alla mattina col fresco, io alla sera dicevo a
loro che io alla mattina dovevo andare a prendere la legna, li
mettevo sul comodino il pane e il formaggio, e quando si
svegliavano mangiavano ma non dovevano uscire fuori dalla
porta perche se uscivano cera l'uomo cattivo, io andavo
presto e per la strada dicevo sempre il rosario, perche anchio
mi mettevo paura, e ritornava verso le 10 quando arrivavo li
trovavo sempre che giocavano, questo lo facevo tante volte
ma forse il Signore mi aiutava, mai mi succedeva niente,
adesso il primo Raffaele aveva 6 anni andava a scuola ma il
secondo Peppino era ancora piccolo, e non cerano asili come
alla prima guerra quando era piccola io, e cosi lo lasciava con i
nonni, era nel mese di novembre e venne unepidemia il tifo
era infettiva Peppino cadde amalato stava male e cosi il primo
Raffaele lo portai da mio padre che non passasse pure a lui il
tifo, Peppino stette male piu di venti giorni non poteva
mangiare niente solo un po' di latte, il tifo non lo prendevano
solo i piccoli perche cerano anche due grandi che una mori
aveva 3 figli, e mori pure una ragazza che era venuta dalla
colombia, allora tante malattie i dottori non li capivano, non
cerano medicine, e neanche latte, tutti quelli che avevano i
malati pagavano un uomo e lo mandavano a un paese vicino
che cerano quelli che avevano le vacche, e si doveva fare meta
aqua e metà latte, mi ricordo che quando non ne potevamo
avere lo facevamo con le mandorle, si pulivano si pestavano
nel mortaio si mettevano nellaqua si filtrava e si davo da bere,
ma il bambino sentiva fame, non mi faceva mai vedere quando
mangiava e gli diceva che non cera nulla, questo durò come ho
detto 20 giorni, mi ricordo che era il giorno di Natale e il
bambino si potette mangiare un po' di semolina, ma dopo
pochi giorni che il piccolo si ricominciava a rimettere, cadde
amalato il grande con tutto che non lo avevo tenuto a casa,

cadde amalato lo stesso ma non cosi grave come il fratello,
imaginato come mi sentiva stanca, e tutto questo tempo stava
sempre sola per paura che la prendessero quello che non
lavevano, ma poi passò, e di tutti quello che lo avevano avuto
perché erano molte solo 2 morirono ma erano come ho detto
grandi. mi sono dimenticato che cosa si mangiava ma non solo
durante la guerra ma sempre i bambini si faceva dell'orzo era
come il grano tutti lo seminavano poi si faceva abrustolire si
maginavo e si faceva come si fà il caffe pareva proprio come
caffe se aveva il latte si faceva meta latte e meta orzo si
metteva lo zucchero e pane e si dava ai bambini piccoli e
grande alla mattina, qualche volta si faceva il pane cotto con
olio e aglio e si dava, e qualche volta si dava la pastina cotto
pure con olio e aglio, tutto questo però era meglio di come
dare ai bambini tutte queste cose dolce, perche quelle erano
tutte naturale nell'orzo non cera caffina, a mezzogiorno pane
con qualche altra cosa, e alla sera si cucinava minestre si usava
molto farinagi maccheroni piu spesso ma fatto a mano, non
quelli comprati, si mangiavano quasi tutti i giorni si facevano
diversi come ho detto allinizio come le li avevi imparato mia
madre. di mio marito in guerra non ho piu parlato come ho
detto prima non sapevamo nulla, io non so raccontare tutto,
poi li fecero prigionieri e non sapemmo piu nulla ci
rivolgemmo alla croce rossa e ad altri ma dopo 7 mesi
sapemmo che era prigioniero, un giorno ricevetti una lettera
era tutto cancellata non si capiva una parola e mi spiegarono
che quello che cera scritto non ero buono e percio era tutto
cancellato, ma adesso sapevo almeno che era vivo, poco
tempo dopo ricevetti dagli S. U. una lettera che laveva scritto
lui, io non capivo, dicevo ma se e prigioniero come viene
dallamerica non ricordo da dove, andai da un uomo vicino alla
mia casa che era venuto dall America e mi disse che mio
marito si trovava prigioniero in America che potevo stare

contenta che per lui la guerra era finita prese la mappa degli S.
U. mi fece vedere ma come ho detto che non ricordo mi
sempre che fu preso prigioniero nel 1942 e tutto questo
tempo prima stette un po' in Inghilterra e poi come ho detto
in America, adesso avevo sue notizie piu spesso ma con poche
parole solo stava bene. anche mio fratello Angelo fu prese
prigioniero e nemmeno da lui avevamo notizie, solo del
cappellano sapevamo dove era, ma neanche cosa facevo vi so
raccontare solo che aiutava tutti quelle persone che
scappavano durante i bombardamenti volevo portarli al
convento specialmente i bambini ma i monaci non volevano
perche dicevano che non avevano posti, allora mio fratello li
aiutava come poteva e col suo stipendio che aveva aiutavo a
questi poveri sfollati. noi al paese sempre la stessa vita in
questo tempo, Peppino cadde di nuovo amalato stava cattiva
aveva bronchita e polmonita stava proprio brutto, il dottore
diceva che se la febra alta non bassava non cera da fare, ma
dopo 4 giorno migliorò in questo tempo mori mio suocero era
il 27 febbraio 1943 senza vedere suo figlio tornare, io ai
funerali stava poco perche duravano 3 giorni, perche Peppino
era ancora amalato, poi mia suocera rimase sola veniva spesso
a casa e volevo che noi andassimo a vivere con lei dato che
dove abitavamo io dovevo pagare laffitto ma io dissi che avrei
andato quando era finito l'anno come avevo pagato il fitto, e
cosi nel mese di ottobre andammo a vivere con lei, stetti un
po insieme ma non mi piaceva tanto, cosi la casa era grande la
dividemmo e facemmo due stanze a lei, e 3 a me, stavamo
vicino si aiutavamo uno con l'altro, e cosi andammo avanti
fino che fini la guerra. quando vennero gli alleati gli americani
che l'Italia aveva perduto ci mandavano tante cose per
mangiare per vestire e si stavo un po' meglio, mi ricordo che
mio fratello il cappellano quando veniva al paese portava
tante cosette perche lui era incaricato a distribuire alla gente la

roba che veniva dall'america, la guerra finì nel 1945, io ero in
casa quel giorno e sentii un fracasso fuori tutti gridavano e
uscii e mi dissero che la guerra era finita ma l'Italia come ho
detto laveva perduta non ricordo di preciso ma era alla fine di
agosto settembre, ma era finita tutta la paura che non
morivano piu giovani, adesso si diceva che non troppo a lungo
incomingiavano a venire i prigionieri, e mio marito fu uno dei
primi al mio paese era il 5 ottobre dissi che non stava tanto
bene, e lo mandarono subbito a casa il viaggio da Lioni un
paese un po' lontano da noi lo fece a piedi perche non
potevano passare nessun mezzo perche tutti i ponti delle
strade e della ferrovia erano state rotte con i bombardamenti e
cosi arrivò alle 2 di notte, io quando sentii bussare alla porta
mi misi paura a vedere che era lui non ci credevo, stava
discretamente bene e di tutti quei giovani del paese che erano
partiti non ricordo ne morirono 3, 4 li chiamavano dispersi
ma non tornarono piu, i prigionieri tornarono uno dopo laltro
e cosi finì, l'Italia era distrutta. se prima della guerra non si
poteva vivere, immaggino dopo, cero un po' di roba che
veniva dall'america e si tirava avanti. come ho detto che mio
fratello cappellano durante la guerra aiutava i sfollati e tutti il
suo stipendio lo dava, a loro quando finì la guerra che tornò al
convento i suoi superiori volevano tutti i soldi che aveva
avuto durante la guerra mio fratello dissi che non ne avevo le
avevo dato ai sfollati, e cosi dissero che non cera piu posto
per lui, allora mio fratello non era piu frate ma uno borghese e
se ne ando a Roma e si mise a fare qualche cosa dato che lui
aveva tre lauree, anche mia sorella la mandarono via perche
listituto dove stava era pure dei frati domenicani dove stava
mio fratello e anche lei restò a Roma mio fratello Angelo
venne al paese lui era stato prigioniero in Germania. dopo un
po' di tempo mio marito si rimise a lavorare del suo mestiere
falegname ma non cerano lavori, avevamo due figli adesso

tutte due grande andavano a scuola ma si stava tranquillo non importa che non cera nulla, un po' con la campagna si poteva mangiare, ma il 31 luglio 1946 naque una bambina la mettemmo il nome Beatrice mio marito aveva letto la divina commedia e gli piaceva Beatrice per non far dispiacere alla madre quando fu battezzata gli mise Beatrice Ernestina come sua madre, era una bella bambina e tutte quelli che ci conoscevano cioe i nostri amici le moglie mi venivano a trovare e dicevano dove lo avevamo trovato quel bel nome, Beatrice e nella culla pareva un angelo, ma piangeva spesso e ogni sera per 8 giorni Bianca la levatrice veniva a casa la visitava la metteva nellaqua e cosi non piangeva piu, ma questa volta non aveva potuto fare il corretino come avevo fatto con i due primi figli, perche non cera niente per comprare che cera stata la guerra, una parente di mia cognata che stava in America, io non la conosceva ma mio marito la conosceva mi mandò un bel pacco con tutte biancheria per bambini, cerano tante belle cose che al mio paese non si avevano mai viste, anche la sorella di mio marito mi mando un pacco, perche quasi tutti quelli che avevano qualcuno in America avevano pacchi, perche in Italia non cera niente per la guerra che cera stato, adesso avevamo 3 figli ma si stava male per vivere non cera lavoro il tempo scorreva un po' buono un po' brutto ma nel 1948 il 16 novembre naque unaltra bambina mi ricordo che una nipote di mio marito aveva fatto una lista di nome come la dovevamo chiamare ma io dissi di chiamarla come mia suocera Ernestina, ma mia suocera voleva che la chiamassi come mia madre che era morta e cosi quando fu battezzata lo dettero il nome Ernestina Maria Filomena, Maria Filomena resto alla fonte battesimale perche cosi si usava e resto solo Ernestina, e cosi avevamo 4 figli il primo Raffaele come mio suocero, il secondo Peppino come mio padre, Beatrice e Ernestina come mia suocera e mia

madre, adesso mio marito voleva andare da qualche parte a
lavorare perche in Italia non aveva dove andare, non
conosceva nessuno, si incomincio a parlare del Venezuela, ma
dicevano che non era buono, il clima era troppo caldo la gente
era cattiva si diceva che vivevano come selvaggi era tutto
diferente da noi ma si diceva di azzardare, cera un nipote
lontano di mio marito che era stagnino, ma non avevo lavoro
aveva due figli e si poteva dire che era disperato, e voleva
andare in Venezuela, ma tutti lo sconsigliavano ma volle
andare, e mandò a dire che non era tanto brutto poi andarono
altri due e cosi andò pure mio marito fece le carte e parti era
nel mese di luglio 1949 mi lasco con 4 figli, adesso era sola e
dovette fare tutto come quando cera la guerra, dovevo
lavorare in campagna, e dovevo accudire 4 figli non due, ma
cera mia suocera che quando andavo in campagna li teneva lei,
dato che era vicino e qualche volta le bambine li portavo con
me, i ragazzi andavano a scuola, partirono altri in Venezuela
erano tutti nostri amici, noi moglie facevamo lo stesso come
prima un giorno si andava a lavorare da uno e unaltro giorno
andavamo dall'altro e stavamo insieme ci aiutavamo uno
coll'altro, ma non tutti questi che erano andati in Venezuela
facevano fortuna, e cosi mio marito era uno di questi, non
poteva trovare lavoro, lavorava solo per mantenersi e
aspettava se miglioravano le cose mandava pochi soldi a noi, e
cosi era sempre lo stesso avevo 4 figli i ragazzi andavano a
scuola dovevano andare sempre puliti, non avevano molti
vestiti e per farli andare sempre puliti e ordinati, alla sera li
lavavo, alla mattina li stiravo e andavano puliti ma poi
Raffaele aveva finito le elementari che come ho detto
all'inizio cera sempre solo fino alla 4 classe, io avevo mio
fratello e mia sorella a Roma e lo mandai da loro cosi
comingio le scuole superiori e stava con loro io mandavo
come potevo un po' di soldi e un po' loro e lo tennero a

studiare, alle vacanza venivano tutti e 3 al paese, ma era un
sacrificio, poi arrivo pure Peppino che era finito la scuola, ma
a Roma non poteva andare perché non avevano posto, e fece
la 5 classe privata, fu promosso e mi consigliarono di fargli
fare pure le medie private, cera una maestra che era stata pure
mia amica, era della mia stessa eta ci avevamo sposato lo
stesso anno, la pregai se lo potessi preparare per poi andare a
fare gli esami a Roma, il ragazzo era tanto inteligente si
portava bene, che in un anno fece due classi. Peppino stette
poco a Roma diceva che se suo padre passava negli stati uniti
voleva venire in america. adesso anche mio fratello Angelo
stava a Roma allaviazione, aveva conosciuto una ragazza di
Verona mentre era in guerra, cera il permesso che chi voleva
scrivere a un soldato o mandargli qualche cosa, e questa
ragazza che si chiamava Renata lo scriveva gli mandava
qualche pacco, e cosi quando fini la guerra la cercò si
innamorarono e si sposarono lui aveva avuto il posto a Roma
cosi erano tutti a Roma mio fratello Michelangelo che adesso
non era piu sacerdote aveva avuto il posto al ministero
del'interno, e facevano delle palazine e chi aveva famiglia ne
aveva una, non so come lui ne ebbi una, ma la cedette a suo
fratello che aveva la famiglia, mio marito in Venezuela non
faceva fortuna, e più il governo venezuelano aveva detto che
tutti i stranieri che lavoravano la, o mandavano a chiamare le
famiglie o dovevano andare via, perche i soldi non dovevano
uscire dalla nazione, perche adesso stranieri ce nerano tanti
quasi tutti Italiani. mio marito aveva fatto domanda se
poteva andare al Nord America e doveva aspettare, mi aveva
scritto a me, che dovevo lasciare in Italia ai due ragazzi, e le
due bambine e io dovevo andare da lui, mi doveva richiamare
come sua moglie e figli, ma io non volle andare, perché prima
non volevo lasciare i ragazzi e poi dove andavo con due
bambine il clima non era per loro, e poi se non lavorava come

facevamo per vivere gli dissi che se passava negli S. U. avrei
venuto e cosi dopo tanto tempo arrivo il suo turno, non mi
scrisse dal Venezuela che doveva passare negli [S.U.] ma mi
scrissi da N. Y. che era arrivato negli stati Uniti era da suo
fratello Alessio, era il 18 dicembre 1953 quando scrissi a noi la
lettera la ricevemmo dopo 3 giorni era due giorni prima di
Natale io era cosi preoccupata che era parecchio che non
avevo avuto notizie e quando arrivò la lettera eravamo tutti
contenti specialmente Peppino che non voleva andare piu a
Roma ma in America. dopo le feste passo a Pgh. dove aveva
la sorella l'altro fratello e il cognato, che era pure falegname,
cosi lo aiutò a trovare il lavoro andò con lui a lavorare, e
stava con loro, comincio a fare le carte per noi, io non ero
tanto contento perche doveva lasciare la mia famiglia, e
specialmente mio padre e mia suocera che erano vecchi, anche
loro erano dispiaciuti che andavo via, ma io avevo promesso e
dovevo venire, mi sono dimenticato di dire che l'anno prima
mia cognata e suo marito, cioè la sorella di mio marito,
vennero in Italia e videro la vita che facevo tutti i giorni in
campagna, i ragazzi e le bambine come vivevano cosa si
mangiavano sapeva che mio marito aveva fatto le carte per
N.A. mi dissi che se passava dovevo senzaltro venire in
America e non come avevo fatto che non aveva andato in
Venezuela, mi ricordo che anche mio fratello Angelo mi disse,
che anche loro tutti si dispiacevano che andavo via ma lo
dovevo fare, perche in Italia con 4 figli non li potevo dare
nessuno avenire, il problema era di Raffaele stava studiando
faceva il liceo e voleva restare almeno per finire il liceo, e
cosi restò io fece tutte le carte non appena arrivò l'atto di
richiamo, le terre le diede a qualcuno che li lavorava, la casa
resto a mia suocera che era la sua, quel poco di fornitura un
po' la vendetti e un po' la diedi a chi la voleva, il raccolto lo
vendetti, per fare tutto questo lavorai tanto ma cera peppino

che mi aiutava volentiero, tutte quelle che conoscievo si
dispiacevano che andavo via, le mie amiche due se ne erano
andate in Venezuela, e una aveva partito pure in America,
perche anche il marito era in Venezuela e aveva avuto il visto
prima di mio marito, e percio di amiche ne erano restato
pochi, cerano tutte quelle che gli cucivo i vestiti che si
dispiacevano e non ti dico poi di mia sorella come era
dispiaciuto, quando veniva alle vaganze stava sempre a casa, e
qualche volta veniva pure in campagna a stare con me, e così
dopo che preparai tutto quello che mi poteva portare, ci
preparai nelle casse perché noi partivamo con la nave,
potevamo portare molta roba, e cosi il 30 novembre 1954
partimmo, quando ci salutammo con mio padre piangeva e
dissi che non lo dovevo lasciare, perche io era lunica dei figli
che aveva stato più con lui, anche mia suocera piangeva, ma
io non potevo far niente, dovevo ubbidire a mio marito,
perche anche lui aveva ragione, era stato sempre solo per il
mondo 7 anni in guerra e prigioniero, e 4 anni in Venezuela,
mi ricordo che quando ci mettemmo nella macchina per
partire cera tanta gente, uno dei miei fratelli resto con mio
padre uno venne con noi, e mia sorella venne da Roma a
Napoli per salutarci, lultimo saluto che non ho piu visto
nessuno, restammo due giorni a Napoli per passare tutte le
visite e cosi partimmo lasciando l'italia e tutti i miei cari
specialmente mio figlio Raffaele con la speranza che ci
raggiungesse presto, per me e Beatrice durante il viagio ce la
passammo male specialmente Beatrice, in 10 giorni che durò il
viaggio non mangiò neanche un bicchiere di latte, uno dei
camerieri che ci serviva perche noi eravamo in prima classe,
mi diceva di sforzarla che mangiasse qualcosa se no non ci
arrivava in America, Peppino ed Ernestina se la passavano
bene, non li faceva male il mare, dopo 10 giorni arrivammo a
N.Y. dove ci aspettava mio marito e suo fratello, certo che

nel vedere N.Y. era per noi come un paradiso, quando
sentivamo di parlare non capivamo nulla, restammo a N.Y. 3
giorni e dopo partimmo per Pgh. tutto il giorno nel treno,
quando arrivammo alla stazione di Pgh. cera mio cognato ad
aspettarci, quando arrivammo alla casa cera mia cognata io la
conoscieva perche lanno prima era venuto in Italia, cerano
tutti i suoi figli. mio marito aveva comprato una casetta non
era tanto buona ma durante il tempo che aspettava a noi
laccomodo alla meglio, tutti gli avevano dato qualche cosa e
trovammo tutto prondo, certo non era un granche ma per
incominciare cosi continuammo a lavorare e la finimmo di
accomodarla, come o detto non era tanto buona, ma era
sempre meglio e con piu comodità di quello che avevamo
l'asciato, cera laqua, e il gas, che al paese non lavevamo, anzi
quando noi partimmo stavano facendo la condottura per
portare l'acqua al paese, e cosi comingio per noi la vita nuova,
le bambine subito andarono alla scuola anche Peppino.
Beatrice aveva 8 anni aveva fatto la 3 elementare al paese e la
misero in secondo grado e Ernestina, non aveva fatto niente
perche aveva 6 anni la misero al primo grado, Peppino al 8
grado dato che aveva fatto la media ma subito lo passarono
alle ai scuola, mio marito andava a lavorare e io stavo in casa,
perche non potevo far niente lavoro fuori che non sapevo la
lingua, certo era duro per me quando andavo a far la spese non
andavo mai sola nel primo tempo, ma poi tutto era piu facile
perche al quartiere dove eravamo noi erano quasi tutti Italiani
e nei negozi si parlava pure Italiano incomingiai a conoscere
gente anche loro venuto d'allitalia prima di noi. e poi si dice
che dal brutto al buono subito si passa, ma dal buono al brutto
non subito si abbitua, e noi avevamo venuto dal brutto, percio
si stava molto meglio, ma io pensavo sempre ai miei che
avevo restato in Italia, specialmente a mio figlio e i vecchi,
mandavamo un po' di soldi ai miei fratelli per Raffaele, ma

mio marito non lavorava sempre, non piu di sei mesi l'anno in
inverno non lavorava, ci davano quel poco di disoccupazione
ma eravamo pure 5 persone, e delle volte non abbastava fino
all'altra settimana, cosi Peppino non volle piu andare a scuola
voleva insegnarsi barbiero, dovevo andare 5 mesi a scuola per
barbieri e dopo si mise pure lui a cercare chi lo prendeva per
lavorare e aiuto un po' col suo lavoro, perche nei primi tempo
non stavamo troppo bene ma si stava sempre meglio
potevamo mangiare di piu, e le bambine si potevano bere
quanto latte volevano, perche al paese lo avevano solo quando
stavano male, dall'Italia avevamo notizie che stavano bene e
Raffaele si portava bene a scuola, erano passate quasi 3 anni e
non ancora lo avevano chiamato per la visita per venire in
America, noi eravamo un po' preoccupoato perche se
compiva i 21 anni non avrebbe piu potuto venire,
conosciavamo una signora vicino a noi aveva un fratello che
era congresso a Wascinton e questo signora lo scrissi una
lettera se poteva fare qualche cosa, e questo fu cosi gentile che
rispose di non preoccuparsi che prima che entrava nei 21 anni
avrebbe arrivato, e cosi fu, venne prima dei 21 anni, adesso
per me specialmente il pensiero dell'Italia era un po'
diminuito, come ho detto che aspettavamo Raffaele che
doveva venire in America la casetta era piccola volevamo
comprare unaltra piu grande certo non avevamo soldi si
doveva pagare mensilmente ma ci voleva un po' di anticipo
cosi il fratello di mio marito ci diede in prestito 2 mila dollari
e comprammo una casa piu grande aveva 4 stanze da letto il
posto dove era era meglio e cosi la comprammo nel mese di
marzo in aprile la pulimmo e andammo ad abitare sempre col
pensiero che mio marito stesse bene in salute e di aver lavoro
ma la sfortuna venne e nel mese di novembre proprio la vigilia
della festa mio marito mentre lavorava stavano facendo un
grande garace gli cadde addosso la terra mentre metteva le

forme di legname era il 27 novembre 1957 immagginate che
paura non potevo andare subito il contrattore che mi chiamo
mi disse di non preoccuparmi che non era molto ma lo dissi
per non spaventarmi Peppino era al lavoro non avevo il suo
numero di telefono chiamai a mia cognata ma non potevamo
far niente doveva venire la sera così lo portarono all'ospedale
era lontano e quando fu la sera andammo io e Peppino le
bambine le lasciai a una vicino di casa. quando arrivammo era
tutto fasciato con le gampe aveva graffi sulla faccia
immagginate se avesse successo una disgrazia come avrei
dovuto fare con la casa appena comprata con 4 figli io non
sapevo nulla di questa terra, ma dovevo solo ringraziare il
Signore che aveva venuto così a poco a poco si rimise da quel
ospedale passo a unaltro piu vicino il suo padrone mi pagava la
sittimana come se lavorasse perche la colpa era la sua e
passarono 6 mesi per incominciare a lavorare. in questo
tempo Peppino come ho detto prima che si aveva imparato
barbiere adesso lavorava e aveva conosciuto una ragazza figli
di oriundi Italiani era una brava ragazza e si voleva sposare noi
non trovammo niente in contrario solo che erano molti
giovani ma se si volevano bene, e così si sposò. ma dopo un
po' di tempo mi scrissi mia sorella che mio fratello Angelo
non stava tanto bene, aveva l'ulcera allo stomaco, lo
dovevano operare, fu operato pareva che tutto era andato
bene, ma si sentiva sempre male allo stomaco fu di nuovo
operato aveva il male incurabile, non cera niente che poteva
guarire e dopo 3 mesi di atroce sofferenza il 14 ottobre 1958
mori aveva 43 anni lasciò una bambina di 6 anni, il dolore per
me fu grande e mi ricordo ancora le sue parole, quando disse
che chi sa se ci vediamo unaltra volta, era uno dei miei che se
ne era andato tanto giovane senza vederlo quando stava male
ci scrisse con le sue mani diceva che se lo avessimo potuto
aiutare se qui si trovavano piu medicine meglio, mio marito

andò dal dottore ma disse che con quel male non poteva far
niente, gli mandammo 100 dollari ma poveretto arrivarono
dopo che lui era morto, quella lettera che come era scritta nel
leggerla ti faceva piangere, forse non credete ma la tenni
tanto tempo e ogni tanto la leggevo. certo per tutti loro era
stato un dolore ancora piu forte di me che lo avevano visto
cosi sofrire, mio fratello Michelangelo dalla morte di suo
fratello non era piu quello di prima aveva restato della sua
mente tutte le sofferenze e quando mi scriveva diceva sempre
che pensava a lui, a mio padre non lo fecero sapere nulla della
sua malattia lo seppe dopo volevano che se lo ricordasse
sempre in buona salute che quando andava al paese, si alzava
alla mattina e andava in campagna a vedere tutto, e quando
ritornava portava sempre i frutti freschi, era cosi contento
che si era fatto quella bella passegiata, ma si senti male lo
stesso, lo voleva vedere lo stesso. Raffaele qua aveva riprese
gli studi faceva luniversita ma andava a scuola alla sera e al
giorno lavorava in laboratorio alla stesso universita, aveva la
fidanzata in Italia e non appena aveva fatto un po' di soldi
avrebbe andato a sposarla e cosi venne, ma quando lui era in
Italia fu chiamato alle armi e dopo un mese ritornò in
America e la moglie restò in Italia con i genitori. nel mese di
maggio parti sotto le armi stette 3 mesi nella Georgia e poi lo
mandarono in Germania, dopo un po' di tempo lo raggiunse la
moglie dall'Italia e stesse due anni, in questo tempo fece le
carte per la moglie per venire in America e quando si congedò
vennero insieme. gli anni passavano mio padre sempre al
paese, non gli piaceva a stare a Roma era abituato nella sua
casa, abituato al suo paese, teneva tanti amici, non volevo
lasciare le sue abitudine, e loro ogni tanti andavano, lo
avevano messo una donna che gli andava a fare i servizi, ma
era sempre un pensiero per loro, e cosi il 22 novembre 1964
mori non era malato mori nel sonno come lui sempre dicevo,

e pregava al Signore di farlo morire subito, aveva 86 anni, non
era mai stato ammalato soffriva solo un po' di artrite la sera
avanti della sua morte era stato con i suoi amici, quando lo
seppi fu un altro dolore per me, senza piu vederlo, perche, noi
non potevamo col denaro di andare in Italia, ci voleva solo la
rassegnazione mi accontentavo che non era stato ammalato,
perche io da lontano non lo avrei potuto dare nemmeno un
bicchiere di aqua, aveva fatto tanto per me, e io niente per lui,
adesso erano restato solo mio fratello Michelangelo, e mia
sorella Assunta, e mia cognata con la bambina, erano tutti
dispiaciuti, ma la vita doveva continuare, ognuno faceva il suo
lavoro, mia cognata con la bambina stavano nella casa che
come ho detto prima ce laveva ceduto mio fratello e loro due
stavano in unaltra appartamento insieme, ma non stettero
molto, perche venne la disgrazia di nuovo, era il 3 maggio del
1965 mio fratello mentre andava in ufficio per lavorare, gli
venne un attacco al cuore cadde e mori mentre lo portavano
in ospedale. dopo otto 8 giorni mio figlio che come ho detto
era sposato abbitava solo aveva gia un bambino, e quando
venne a casa per darmi la brutta notizia, non sapeva come
dire, perche avevano passato appena 7 mesi dalla morte di
mio padre, si mise a piangere e io capii subito che cera
unaltra cattiva notizia, mi dissi che Michelangelo non cera
piu, era morto con un attacco al cuore, non potete credere,
che dispiacere io due giorni prima avevo avuto una sua lettera
dove mi raccomandava per la mia salute, dato che io ho la
pressione alta, mi diceva di star attenta a che dovevo
mangiare, che lui stava bene e la sua pressione e piu bassa che
alta, anche questa sua ultima lettera la conservai come quella
dell'altro fratello, anche lui se ne aveva andato giovane aveva
55 anni adesso era restato solo Assunta, qui tutto procedeva
un po' buono un po' brutto i ragazzi si erano sposato avevano
i figli e ognuno lavorava non vi ho detto che Raffaele stette

due anni in germania e quando torno andò a finire la scuola
prese il diploma di chimica prese il lavoro alla golfo e dove
lavoro tuttora Peppino da barbiere e stanno bene, le ragazze
ormai alle scuole superiore. in questo tempo anche mia
suocera mori era vecchia aveva 95 anni ma lei mori di
vecchiaia mi dispiaque cera con lei un altro figlio che era
andato in Italia ma ci rassegnammo a pensare che quando una
muore vecchio non tanto e brutto perche lo sappiamo che
dobbiamo morire, mio marito sta bene con quelle che e passto,
certo sente sempre qualche dolore e lavora, come sempre ho
detto che lavoro solo 6 mesi all'anno, io sto in casa la mia
salute non e male, sto sotto cura vado spesso dal dottore a
controllare la pressione, sto in casa faccio tutto come mi
insegnava mia madre, cucino faccio il pane, faccio i
maccheroni a mano, cuce qualche cosa per me, non mi sono
mai comprato un vestito me li faccio da me, lavoro con
l'uncinetto con i ferri, lavoro nel giradino taglia l'erba, coltiva
i fiori, coltiva lorto, perche abbiamo molta terra intorno alla
casa e facciamo pomodori peperoni verdura e faggioli e li
metti nei barattoli per l'inverno e cosi passa il tempo, con
mia sorella ci scriviamo, certo e sola. lavora dice che sta bene,
pensa che vorrebbe comprarsi un appartamento che a Roma
sono un po' scarse le case e l'affitto e alto, dice che dove
abbita il padrone e vecchio e la vuole vendere, e se la vuole
comprare, dopo un po' di tempo era nel mese di settembre ci
scrive che la comprata a messo un po' di soldi avanti e il resto
lo pacherà mensilmente ma non ebbi fortuna, dopo 2 mesi
mentre era in una conferenza nel suo lavoro non si sentiva
bene subito la portarono all'ospedale gli aveva venuto un
attacco cerebrale stette 20 giorni allospedale ma il 13
novembre 1969 mori, aveva avuto il trombosi celebrale,
quando arrivò la notizia a mio figlio, dato che lui aveva i
genitori della moglie a Roma sempre a lui scrivevano, cosi

venne a casa non sapeva come dirmelo ma io capii che era una
cosa male che mi doveva dire, mi mise a piangere era finita la
mia famiglia non aveva piu nessuno tutti morti mia sorella
anche lei giovane aveva 49 anni, in 10 anni la mia familia era
tutta morta, io non avevo voglia piu di far niente pensavo
sempre a loro, e dicevo che fra poco anchio me ne dovevo
andare, ma piano piano mi rassegnai cera restata solo mia
cognata e mia nipote, mio marito dopo un po' di tempo ando
in Italia per vedere, perche come ho detto cerano terre al
paese, cera la casa che mia sorella aveva comprata, poveretta
non aveva avuto neanche il tempo per finirla di mettere a
posto, adesso si doveva rivenderla per pagare il debito che
aveva fatto per comprarla, io non volle andare erano tutti
morti e non mi sentivo di andare feci la procura a mio marito
e andò lui se poteva fare qualche cosa, con mia cognata perche
anche lei che rapresentava la figlia era erede, io era restata ma
mi sentivo morta pure con loro, e pensavo a quando bene mi
avevano tutti fatti. quando tenevano i miei figli con loro,
specialmente a Raffaele che era stato con loro fino a quando e
venuto in America, e anche lui se li ricorda sempre. nel 1971
mi venne un desiderio di vedere qualcuno dei miei, ma in Italia
non volle andare, avevo una cuggina di padre e madre, perché
mia madre e sua madre si erano sposati a due fratelli eravamo
cuggine proprio di un sangue questa stava nel Venezuela e disse
a mio marito che volevo andare almeno per otto giorni e
andammo, poveretta anche lei aveva il marito che non stava
tanto bene, aveva il diabete ma non era cosi male aveva una
piccola piaga al piede che non guariva mai che con diabete
dicono che non guarisci, ma nel 1972 nel mese di aprile dopo
tante sofferenze mori da quella piaga sviluppo il cangro e mori
anche lui giovane aveva 2 figli, da quel momento mio marito
si inbresionò tanto, questo era anche stato uno dei suoi amici
era proprio uno di quelli giovani come ho detto prima che

facevano finto di dormire e venivano da noi alla sera, allora
mio marito mi dissi, che volevo andare in Italia e doveva
andare pure io, che se non andavamo non avremmo andato
piu, io lo accontentai e nel mese di maggio del 1973
andammo, ci aspettava mia cognata, non cera nessuno dei
miei fratelli e sorella non i miei genitori e neanche quelli di
mio marito, come arrivammo a Roma il giorno dopo subbito
andammo al cimitero a portare i fiori che dispiacere a vedere
le loro fotografie vicino alle tombe cosi giovane, specialmente
mio fratello Michelangelo con quel sorriso, perche lui rideva
sempre, e diceva a noi tutti quando eravamo arrabiato, di non
arrabiarci perche la vita e breve, come lo avessi saputo che
doveva morire giovane, poi andammo al paese e anche qui
prima di tutto andammo al cimitero a vedere le tombe dei
nostri genitori, restammo in Italia 45 giorni sempre il giro a
vedere i santuari quelli che eravamo andati quando eravamo
giovani, andammo da Milano Venezia Pisa Firenze Roma
Napoli Pompei Capri Sorrento Salerno Avellino passammo
tutti quei paesi che qualcuno eravamo stai come Caposele
Materdomini qui ci fermammo 3 giorni che cera un grante
santuario S. Gerardo Maiella che e tanto famoso da quelle
parte e poco distante dal nostro paese passammo nelle Puglie
Foggia sul Monte Gargano, al paese restammo poco, non cera
piu nessuno dei nostri amici cera qualche cuggino tutti erano
andati via chi all'estero e chi in alta Italia per lavoro. quasi
tutti a Torino cosi andammo a Torino quasi solo per vedere a
loro, io avevo due stretti cuggini con le loro famiglie, cerano
pure qualche amico della nostra gioventù, e solo a Torino mi
sentii un poco con i miei di famiglia ci restammo 8 giorni a
Roma stavamo con mia cognata mi sentiva male che non cera
nesuno dei miei fratelli e mia sorella restammo 2 giorni con i
genitori di mia nuora Anna, loro avevano venuto in America
dalla figlia e li avevamo conosciuti e dopo 45 giorni

ritornammo in America, non piansi quando partii dall'italia
per tornare in america tanto non lasciavo nessuno, anzi mi
pareva mille anni che arrivava a casa a vedere tutti i miei figli
mio marito si rimise a lavorare, ma lavorò poco tempo uno o
2 anni, perché non si sentiva piu di lavorare aveva 62 anni e
andò in pensione, io lo stesso come prima con tutte le mie
faccende di casa, ma adesso che mio marito non lavorava piu
si interessò lui in giardino a tagliare lerba e altri lavori ma
nell'orto lo piantavo io che tante cose non le sapeva fare, il
tempo scorreva come sempre, le due ragazze ormai grande
andavano ancora a scuola in universita i due figli avevano le
loro famiglie e tutti alle loro case, adesso anchio avevo 62
anni e anchio aveva la pensione, certo era quella che mi
aspettava del lavoro che aveva fatto mio marito perche io
non avevo lavorato in nessun posto, la mia salute non e piu
come prima non so se ho detto che ho la pressione alta ma
adesso si e agiunta anche l'asma non posso respirare sono
stata 4 volte in ospedale, ma questo male non passa si
mantiene solo con le medicine, ma quando sto discretamente
faccio tutto come sempre, mio marito mi dice che non sto
mai ferma, io gli rispondo che chi si ferma e morta e
continuo, delle volte mi arrabio che lui non si muove e
potrebbe fare di piu, gli piace molto leggere e quello fa, ma
adesso siamo rimasti soli noi due, le ragazze finiti le scuole se
ne sono andate per lavoro sono andate in N.Y. in Long Island
non si sono sposate, i due figli maschi non sono in citta come
noi ma si sono comprate le case fuori citta ma non sono
lontani e ogni settimana ci vediamo, stanno bene anno 3 figli
ciascuno, il primo a due femmine e un maschio il secondo ne
ha 3 femmine anche mia cognata l'anno scorso e morta non
ce e restato piu nessuno mia nipote se e sposata, ma e stata
sempre indiferente con noi, noi sempre abiamo mandato
qualche cosa ci facemmo un bel regalo quando si sposò ci

scriviamo poco, nel 1980 il 23 novembre fece il terremoto in
Italia proprio dalle nostre parti cioe nella provincia di
Avellino dove si trova il mio paese che fu danneggiato il 50
per cento, fummo cosi dispiaciuto fortunatamente non vi
furono vittime, ma mio marito sempre che aveva il desiderio
di vedere come era stato danneggiato, ma quest'anno non ha
potuto piu resistere del desiderio di vedere il nostro paese, e
cosi a deciso di andare, io non ci posso andare perche come ho
detto che o l'asma che mi da tanto fastidio, e poi non ho piu
nessuno, dovrei andare di nuovo a vedere le loro tombe ci
avrei pure andato ma per la salute che non possa, e meglio che
ricordo il mio paese come lo lasciai 28 anni fa, bello pulito
ridente su una collina 815 metro al livello del mare con unaria
pulita e chiara che da un lato al mattino ce l'aurora quando
sorgeva il sole e alla sera al tramonto il sole calava con quei
raggio di fuoco,e alla notte la luna con le stelle che brillavano
erano cosi chiare li contavamo sempre quando eravamo
bambini, sono 28 anni che mi trovo qui in America non ho
mai potuto vedere il cielo azzurro con il sole che splende
pulito e neanche ho mai visto la notte bella con la luna chiare
e le stelle, alla primavera quando arrivavano a migliaia le
rondini dalle parti calde con il loro canto come se volessero
dire siamo arrivate, e in autunno quando si mettevano in fila
sui fili eletrici col loro canto per dirci arrivederci all'anno
prossimo per poi ripartire di nuovo ai luoghi caldi, perche da
noi veniva l'inverno, il mio paese era povero ma bello, non
credete che io lo volli lasciare con piacere, avevo vissuto fino
a 43 anni, ma lo volle lasciare per i figli, e cosi adesso mio
marito e andato a vederlo in compagnia con mia figlia
Beatrice io mi trovo qui in Long Island con laltra figlia
Ernestina mi piace a star qui prima che sto con loro e qiusto,
ma mi manga una cosa pare che qui i giorni sono sempre lo
stesso non ce domenica, per me la domenica consiste che devo

andare alla messa, sono abituata e pare che per me la
domenica se non vado a messa non ho fatto tutto, mi manga
una cosa, mi ricordo che quando eravamo bambini, se qualche
volta non ci volevamo andare, mia madre diceva chi non va a
messa non mangia, il paese era così religioso a pensare che
cerano quelli che abitavano in campagna durante il freddo e la
neve venivano ogni domenica alla messa, qui non ci vado e la
chiesa e lontana, il mondo e campiato, la fede la gente di oggi
la messa da parte, si pensa solo a far male uccidere rubare non
ce piu pudore, si puo dire che sono piu corretti gli animali, chi
sa se tutto questo non e la condotta che tengono le persone,
che Iddio ci castiga. Iddio quando creò il mondo lo fece bello,
ma noi che lo abitiamo labbiamo fatto cattivo, la mia storia e
finita. questo che ho detto dallinizio e tutto vero, ci sono
tante cose che con la mente me le ricordo, ma non le so
scrivere, perche non ho cultura, fece 60 anni fa la quarta
classe in un piccolo paese come ho detto allinizio con mia
madre ammalata, ora mi mancano 3 mesi per compire 70
anni, o tanto lavorato o avuto tanti dispiaceri, ma sono
ancora su questa terra, il mio destino non era come i miei
fratelli e la mia sorella che se ne sono andati tutti giovani
come anche mia madre che aveva appena 53 anni, e aveva
tanto sofferta, domani se Iddio vuole arriva mio marito
dall'Italia con mia figlia e mi raccontano tutto, ma e meglio a
non saperlo. fra 8 giorni ritorniamo a Pgh. dove mi aspettano
i miei figli e nipoti e anche il gatto, poveretto stava sempre
con me chi sa come mi cerca, prendere di nuovo le mie
abitudine, a pulire la casa andare in giardino alla messa alla
domenica, e tante altre cose, sola che mi dispiace a lasciare di
nuovo alle mie figlie lontane, ma la vita e fatta così. anchio
lasciai mio padre e tutti i miei cari per non vederli mai piu.

ABOUT THE AUTHORS

LEONILDE FRIERI RUBERTO was born in Cairano (province of Avellino, Italy) in 1913. She completed the fourth grade, married, worked, and raised four children before she and her family emigrated to Pittsburgh, Pennsylvania, in 1954. She died in Sound Beach, New York in 2000. Encouraged by one of her daughters, and prompted in part by the destruction of her home village in the 1980 Irpinia Earthquake, she wrote her life's story.

LAURA E. RUBERTO, a 2006 Fulbright scholar, teaches film studies at Berkeley City College, where she co-chairs the Department of Arts and Cultural Studies. She authored *Gramsci, Migration, and the Representation of Women's Work* (Lexington/Rowman & Littlefield, 2007) and co-edited *Italian Neorealism and Global Cinema* (Wayne State UP, 2007). Her translation of Umberto Postiglione's "Like Falcons" appears in the upcoming American edition of Francesco Durante's *Italianamerica* (Fordham UP).

Ilaria Serra is assistant professor of Italian at Florida Atlantic University, where she teaches Italian cinema, Italian American cinema, Italian Literature, and Italian language. Her research spans from Italian cinema and literature to the history of Italian immigration to the United States. She is the author of *Immagini di un immaginario: L'emigrazione italiana negli Stati Uniti fra i due secoli: 1890–1925* (CIERRE, 1997); *The Value of Worthless Lives: Writing Italian American Immigrant Autobiographies* (Fordham UP, 2007); and *The Imagined Immigrant. Images of Italian Emigration to the United States between 1890 and 1924* (Fairleigh Dickinson UP, 2009).